A Matter of Motive

By Margot Kinberg

Grey Cells Press

A Matter of Motive

Copyright © 2019 by Margot Kinberg

This is a work of fiction. Names, characters, businesses, places, events and incidents are either the products of the author's imagination or used in a fictitious manner. Any resemblance to actual persons, living or dead, or actual events is purely coincidental.

Cover art Copyright © 2019 by Lesley Fletcher
Visit http://www.lesleyfletcher.com/ for more information about her work

Dedication

Like everything I do, this book is dedicated to my family.

Acknowledgements

I am very grateful to Lynn Mancini, whose editing skill, suggestions, and polishing helped make this this novel so much more than it was. I value her skills, and more, than that, her friendship.

I'd also like to thank Cat Connor for giving me useful insights. This book is much the better for her help.

Thanks also to Lesley Fletcher, whose artwork graces this cover. Her art is elegant and adds a special touch of beauty to my work. Her friendship enriches me.

A final heartfelt thanks to the many members of the writing community and the crime fiction community. You have all taught me so much, and I am privileged to be one of you.

About *A Matter of Motive*…

A man is dead in his car, slumped over the steering wheel. But who killed him? Ron Clemons is the last person you'd think would be murdered. His wife and son love him. His employees respect him. His business is doing well. His clients seek him out. But someone wanted him dead.

The Clemons case is a golden opportunity for newly minted police detective Patricia Stanley to prove herself. It's her first murder investigation, and she wants to do well. But it's not going to be easy. For one thing, she has plenty to learn about handling a murder. And nearly everyone involved in this one is hiding something. Patricia faces her own challenges, too, as the investigation brings back the murder of an old love.

"*A Matter of Motive* hooked me from the first sentence and drew me into a world peppered by grief, danger, friendship, family, and a motive for murder. The characters are believable and human in their frailty and strengths."

- Cat Connor author of The Byte Series

Table of Contents

One 6

Two 25

Three 47

Four 68

Five 88

Six 110

Seven..128

Eight 152

Nine...166

Ten...188

Eleven..205

Twelve 231

Thirteen...245

Fourteen 260

Fifteen..281

Sixteen 293

One

The pain started as Ron buckled his seat belt. At first, he didn't pay very much attention to it. He was middle-aged now, and aches and pains were starting to be a part of daily life. And he'd started his exercise program yesterday. Still, he felt fine that morning as he went to his office. It was a regular Wednesday morning, like so many others. Stop for coffee, get to the office, catch up with email, return telephone calls, and then a conference with Emma about his schedule for the day. After that a meeting with some of the people at the office, that was all. Everything normal. Must be he just bent the wrong way as he got into the car.

No, he'd done more than just twist a muscle or hurt a joint. The pain got worse – a lot worse – as he pulled out of the company's parking lot and joined the westbound traffic on Lancaster Avenue. Maybe it was an anxiety attack. He wasn't normally that type, but with everything that had happened lately, who knew? Should he stop at the urgent care place? No, he didn't have time for that. You could wait a lifetime at those places before anyone saw you. Besides, it wasn't that long a drive from Paoli to Haverford; he'd just open the windows and breathe slowly. That would help. And there wasn't a lot of fast traffic on this road. Not like there was on the Schuylkill Expressway. He'd be all right.

And he was, for a minute or two. Then the pain on the left side of his chest suddenly got worse. He'd never had heart trouble before, but this damned well felt like the heart attack symptoms he'd read about in those pamphlets they always had at doctors' offices. And he'd heard about people who'd been healthy all of their lives suddenly having heart attacks. No, wait, maybe this wasn't serious. Now he was feeling a little better. He was being ridiculous. Breathe deeply. There, even better. He'd call his doctor for an appointment as soon as he got done with this meeting.

And hopefully the meeting wouldn't take long. It absolutely had to come first, though. Spenglar Galleries was branching out from their New York City home and was planning to open a gallery and showroom in nearby Haverford. They were interested in hiring his publicity company for a campaign and if there was one thing he didn't want to do, it was to ruin this opportunity. A successful campaign for Spenglar could lead to some major accounts and do a lot to enhance his company's reputation. And being sloppy about the meeting was the best way to scuttle this deal before they'd even started the campaign. Everything else, including how he was feeling, was just going to have to wait.

For another short while he concentrated on driving, slowly and carefully. Good, the pain was a little less. He started to sweat but did his best to ignore it. He didn't want to cause an accident and besides, a little sweat was the least of his problems. Then the pain hit again; this time it was even worse than it had been. Focus, focus, focus. Steer, watch the road, don't panic. The campaign is going to be great. Think about that. Get to Spenglar. Make them happy. The deal, the deal, the deal. The pain will go away. It did, too, before it started up again. This time it was his arm, too. When he began to feel dizzy, he knew he was going to have to pull over. He didn't want to miss his meeting, but there was nothing he could do. A few minutes by the side of the road and he might be OK anyway. He could call the Spenglar people once he'd rested for a minute. Steer, steer. Focus. There! There was a decent place to pull over. The Meridian Bank parking lot. That would do. His phone. Where was his phone? He unlocked the door and looked down to see if it had fallen between the seat and the door. It had. With a last effort, he stretched his hand down for it, but he couldn't reach it.

"Did you just see that?" Terri asked.

"What, the guy in the Infiniti?" Shawn said.

"Yeah. What the hell was that about? He was driving crazy! He just cut you off!"

"I don't know. Whatever. He's pulled over now. Maybe he's drunk or something."

"This early? Maybe we should call someone. What if something's wrong?"

"Who are we supposed to call? The cops? He'll wake up feeling like an idiot and then lose his license or something. Maybe he's just asleep."

"What if he's hurt? What if he needs an ambulance?"

"Damn it, Terri, you know I don't have my license yet. As it is, we're not in school. If I get caught with Dad's car, we're both fucked."

"Oh, Christ, Shawn, pull over and call the damned cops! Say it's an anonymous caller. Whatever. Just stop being such a baby!"

"Fine! Next parking lot. Just shut up a second and let me think."

"Look, there's the drugstore. Pull over there."

Shawn nodded and pulled into the drugstore's
parking lot. He stared out the window while Terri
called 9-1-1, and then he lit up a cigarette while she
told the dispatcher what she'd seen. Yes, the car
was pulled over. No, it wasn't in the middle of the
road. Some kind of black car. An Infiniti, she
thought. No, she didn't know the driver. She had no
idea of the address. Yeah, on Lancaster Avenue.
The Meridian Bank parking lot. No, that was really
all she knew. No, she didn't want to give her name.
Finally, she got off the phone.
"You done now? Can we just get out of here?"

Seven minutes later, the ambulance roared into
Meridian's parking lot. A few customers who were
getting out of their cars stopped to watch. Faces
started appearing in the bank windows too as the
paramedics jumped out, grabbed a stretcher and
rushed towards the black Infiniti with the driver
slumped down in the front seat. Thank God the key
was sill in the car's ignition, so the door was
unlocked. That made everything easier. After a few
words, the paramedics eased the driver out of the
seat and carefully onto the waiting stretcher. They
bundled the patient into the back of the ambulance
and left with the siren screaming. Paoli Memorial
wasn't far away, and it had a top trauma center. The
weather was cloudy but at least it was dry.
Hopefully the guy would make it.

It was the silence that hit Rachel the hardest as she
moved from room to room. She and Ron shared this
home for twenty-five years and she'd gotten

accustomed to the sounds of another person living in the same place. The clink of his keys on the pine table in the hallway as he came in, the thud of his shoes when he took them off, the soft buzz of the TV, they were all woven through her life. They were the sounds of life, really. Now the silence was going to take over. She would have to get used to it.

For a full twenty minutes she sat motionless on the overstuffed tan leather chair in the living room. His chair. The one he'd always sat in. The hell with what she was going to do with the rest of her life – what was she going to do in an hour?

She nearly jumped as her telephone vibrated on the seat beside her. She didn't want to talk but she knew that if she ignored it, Lina would keep calling until she answered.

"Hi, Lina."

"Rachel! I was afraid you wouldn't pick up. Did you make it home OK?"

"I'm here, don't worry."

"You should have let Kyle and me drive you. You shouldn't be alone right now."

You don't get it, do you, Rachel thought. Alone is exactly what I need to be right now. But she knew her sister meant well. "I made it home. And honestly, I want some time alone. I'm totaled."

"Fine, but I'm going to stop over later – just to make sure you're OK."

"All right," Rachel said.

A glance at her watch – how stupid! As though it really mattered what time it was – told her that it had only been three and a half hours since the telephone call. Mrs. Clemons, they'd said, could you please come right away? There's been an accident. She'd run two red lights, but she hadn't gotten to the hospital soon enough. Ron was dead by the time she arrived – dead, they said, of a heart attack. A massive coronary; we're very sorry, we did everything we could.

Someone in a volunteer uniform had steered her towards a 'Family Privacy' room. It wasn't luxurious but at least you could shut the door. "Can I call someone for you? Get you something?" the girl had asked. Her voice sounded far away, the way a voice sounds when you're under water.
"No, thanks. I just want to sit for a few minutes."
Three and a half hours later, Rachel still just wanted to sit.

At the Paoli offices of Mid-Atlantic Publicity Services, Emma Yeats hung up the telephone, her face strained and tired. That was the second time they'd called from the gallery office where her boss was supposed to have been at a meeting three hours ago. Not that he was perfect, but he was pretty good at getting to meetings and so on. She'd never felt that he needed babysitting. Things like this made the company look sloppy, and it just wasn't like her boss to do that. She'd managed to persuade them that an emergency meeting had come up, but the truth was that she had no idea what had happened to him.

She thought for a moment and then decided to call his wife. Emma didn't want to scare Mrs. Clemons, but maybe she knew where her husband was.

"Hello?" The voice seemed distant, almost like a memory of a voice rather than a real one.

"Rachel? It's Emma Yeats at the office."

"Oh, my God! I'm so sorry! I didn't think – I should have – you don't know yet, do you?"

"Know what?" Emma's stomach muscles clenched. This sounded bad.

"Ron. It's Ron. He's – I'm sorry to have to tell you over the phone, Emma. He's dead."

"Dead?"

"Yes, I just got back from the hospital. It was a heart attack. He was on his way to a meeting. He collapsed. I'll have to get his car. It's still by the side of the road. Maybe I'll…"

"Look, don't even think about that right now. I'll call a tow service. Let me at least do that."

"Will you? Yes, that will help. Thanks."

Rachel put the telephone next to her on the seat again. She hadn't even noticed that her tears had gotten it wet.

Patricia Stanley stood next to the dark blue late-model Infiniti parked by the side of Lancaster Avenue. It was only a two-lane road, but still, how the hell the guy had had the presence of mind to pull over she didn't know. She was glad, though. At least nobody else had been involved in this accident. She made a few notes in the pocket notebook she always carried with her and then glanced up. The heavy clouds that had rolled in this morning were still there, but at least it hadn't started to rain. Still, there was an unmistakable hint of lingering winter in the air even though it was March. She hunched her shoulders under her police-

issue jacket, flipped her blonde ponytail so it fell
outside the jacket collar, and looked across the car
"Hey, Luke," she called to her partner. "You think
that guy made it?"

"Dunno," Luke answered. "He looked pretty
damned bad."

Patricia walked over to the other side of the car so
she wouldn't have to raise her voice.

"The paramedics said it looked like a heart attack."

"Looked that way to me. I don't have my EMT
training – just the emergency first aid classes the
academy offered. But still."

"Yeah, I think you're right. Hope he lives. Can't
believe he got over to the side of the road."

They both looked up when a loud rumble
announced the arrival of a tow truck. The driver got
out of the cab and walked over to the car.

"This it?" he asked himself out loud. "Yup, dark
blue Infiniti. Westbound on Lancaster. That's what
she said."

"That's what who said?" Patricia asked.

"Sorry, Officer. I got a call from …" he looked
down at his clipboard, "Emma Yeats. She's a
secretary over at Mid-Atlantic Publishing. Said this
was her boss' car and it needed to be towed to his
house. I told her I'm not allowed to do that if it's
not her car. But she asked me if I could at least go
see if it's there. So I figured, I'm coming this way,
anyway, I'll just take a look."

"She say anything else?" Luke asked.

The driver turned towards him. "She said the guy
died."

'Shit!' Luke cursed and ran his hand through his
thick afro. The driver nodded. "Look," he said, "If

you want me to take this, I'm gonna need paperwork."

"Go ahead," Patricia said. "We'll OK it. Give me the address, though, will you?"

"Yeah, all right."

The two officers took one last walk around the car as the driver got ready to hitch it up to his truck. Nothing on the ground they needed. Patricia took a few pictures of the scene, just in case. She was still new enough with the Malvern Police Department that she didn't want to screw anything up. She walked back to the cab of the tow truck, where the driver was getting ready to lower the boom. Leaning one arm on the open window, she asked, "Who called you guys again?"

"Name's Emma Yeats. Mid-Atlantic Publicity Services."

"Thanks." She nodded and wrote the name down in her notebook. Then she backed away as the Infiniti was slowly hitched up to the tow truck. She waited with Luke until the truck had slowly pulled into the westbound traffic on Lancaster Avenue.

When the truck had gone, Luke said, "I'm going to call Dispatch and let them know we're going over to the hospital. We'll need their intake for our report."

"Sounds good. Thanks."

While Luke called into the police station, Patricia flipped through her notes. It looked like she had everything she needed.

"You ready?" she asked when Luke had finished.

"Yeah, let's go. And after this, I want some lunch. You're buying this time."

"Bullshit, Enders! I bought last time." She gave him a mock shove as he started the police unit.

Paoli Hospital wasn't a huge hospital, but it was well-equipped and had a good trauma center. When Patricia and Luke got there, they ID-d themselves to the Emergency Services receptionist. She took their names and asked them to wait.

Patricia glanced around at the clean, bright waiting area. She'd been here a few times since she joined the Malvern PD, but she never found it easy.

"What's wrong with you?" Luke asked. "Never seen a waiting room before? We've been here a few times."

Patricia shook her head, annoyed with herself. "I'm fine," she said. "Just not a big fan of hospitals. Let's just sit down.

After about ten minutes, one of the doctors came towards them, extending a hand when he got close enough. He looked like a resident – early thirties, thinning brown hair cut short, and wire-rimmed glasses. He wore a rumpled white coat and it looked as though he hadn't had enough sleep in about a month.

"I'm Dr. O'Brien – Steve O'Brien. How can I help you?"

"Thanks for seeing us," Patricia said. "We're here about a patient who came in earlier. A heart attack case. We need some information to finish up our paperwork."

"Do you know the name?"

"Clemons. Ronald Clemons. Age 55."

O'Brien led them to a large station next to the receptionist's desk. He opened a small gate, went through it to the other side of the station and in a moment called up the records he wanted.

"Here it is. Clemons, Ronald. Yes, he had a severe myocardial infarction. Died before we could do much of anything for him. He's due to be autopsied in a couple of hours."

"Thanks," Luke said. "Let us know if anything comes up, OK?" He slid one of his cards across to O'Brien.

"Will do. Looks routine, but we won't know anything until after the autopsy."

The two officers thanked him and walked back the way they'd come, through the waiting room and towards the Emergency Services entrance.

For the next two days Rachel went through the motions of being alive one movement at a time. Even getting dressed, making coffee or tea and talking on the telephone were monumental efforts. People stopped over, dropped things off, left. Faces in and out of the house. I'm so sorry, what can we do, is there anything you need? The doorbell rang. The telephone rang. Mail was delivered. Rachel saw everyone and everything through a haze. Lina came, stayed for hours, went home, came back. She told Rachel when to eat, when to sleep, when to take the sedative the doctor had given her. Rachel had always chafed against Lina's habit of knowing what was best, but right now it was welcome. Thinking on her own was too hard. Remembering wasn't possible right now. No, she couldn't do that.

On Friday morning Rachel stumbled from the bedroom to the bathroom, still thick-headed and stupid from the sleeping pill. She felt clumsy, but it was better than actually feeling. After she used the bathroom, she splashed cold water on her face and looked into the mirror. The woman who looked back at her had matted, curly chestnut hair that hadn't been washed, blue circles under her eyes and a haggard look around her cheeks and mouth. Empty eyes stared at her. Who was that ghost? Clean up. Try to shower and dress today. Yes, I can do that. Maybe.

A faint noise from the kitchen brought her back. Lina had stayed overnight and must be getting ready to make breakfast. The thought of eating made Rachel feel a little sick, but Lina would insist. And she was right. Feeling light-headed from not eating just made things worse. She would try to eat a piece of toast or something. And anyway, the kitchen was the sunniest room in the house, always had been. That's the way Rachel had wanted it. It made her feel more alive. Yes, the kitchen would be a good place to sit. Cream-and-beige cabinetry, stainless steel fixtures, and yellow curtains on the windows. Sunlight streamed in when the weather was nice. It was cloudy today, and the forecast was for rain, but still, the kitchen would make her feel better. She slowly left the bathroom. Down the hall, the kitchen is on the right. It'll be warm there and bright, and Ron will be reading the paper. No, not Ron. Lina will be there. Not Ron. She walked slowly, one foot, then another. Walk to the kitchen.

Lina looked up from the paper as Rachel came in. "You're awake."
"Looks like it." Not awake. A zombie.
"We need to go to the funeral home today."

"I know. I look like hell. I need a shower. I need to put some clothes on. I will. Later."
Lina tried to get her to help decide which of the many donated meals to thaw for dinner. Not that it mattered. Rachel couldn't taste anything anyway.
"Whatever you want, Lina, OK? I don't care." That was when Rachel's telephone rang.

"Hello?"
"Is this Rachel Clemons?"
"Yes. Who's this please?" She heard herself saying the words as though she were listening to someone else.
"This is Dr. Monique Travers from Paoli Memorial Hospital." The hospital. Ron lying, white and quiet, under the sheet. Yes, that is my husband.
"Yes? Is there – do you –" Say something, you idiot, Rachel told herself. Have a damned conversation.
"I'm with the pathology department here at the hospital, and I have a couple of questions about your husband. Do you have a minute?"
"OK." Rachel slowly sat down on one of the two yellow faux-leather barstools next to the kitchen's island workspace. Lina hovered near, but Rachel waved her away, pointing at the coffee pot next to the stove. Lina nodded and got to work.
"Was your husband taking any medication at the time of his death?"
"You mean prescription medication?"
"That's what I mean, yes."
"Not that I know of. He wasn't sick or anything if that's what you mean."
"No medication at all?"

[18]

She heard the soft chink of cups and saucers as Lina made the coffee. Things came into focus and went out of focus again.

"Mrs. Clemons?"

"Sorry. It's…very difficult right now."

"I know it must be, and I'm sorry to have to bother you at a time like this, but –"

"– Then why the hell are you! Oh, God, I'm sorry! I didn't mean that! I'm just…I'm a mess." Lina turned away from the kettle for a moment, her eyebrows raised. Rachel shook her head.

"I know this is awful for you. If you'd rather me call back later, I can do that."

"No, let's get it over with. Why did you ask me about Ron's medications?"

"Your husband died of a heart attack, but we didn't see any signs of heart disease. There are some medications that can mimic a heart attack in certain patients. I was wondering whether your husband might have been taking one of them."

"Oh, I see." Ron eating breakfast, vitamins next to his plate of toast. Sips from her coffee cup as she looked over at him. The smell of the toast. No, that was Lina making toast. "No, I don't think he was taking anything. Only over-the-counter multi-vitamins. Sometimes he took aspirin for a headache or backache. That's all. Is there a problem?"

"We're just trying to tie up some loose ends, Mrs. Clemons, that's all."

"Right, of course." The doctor's voice went on, fading into the background. More apologies for the intrusion. Condolences, as though that mattered. Thank you for your time, we'll be in touch, good bye.

"What was that about?" Lina asked as she placed a yellow-and-white striped china cup in front of Rachel. She pushed the sugar in Rachel's direction too.

"A doctor. From the hospital. Something about pathology and what medications Ron was taking." She put sugar in the coffee and stirred it, then took a sip. She blinked a little as the hot liquid scalded her mouth.

"Here," Lina pushed a box of tissues towards her sister. "You're crying again, honey."

"I am?"

The mood in the small conference room at Mid-Atlantic Publicity Services was as dismal as the March rain outside. The five people at the round yellow oak table looked quickly at each other and then just as quickly away. Ron Clemons' seat was still there, empty. Nobody looked in that direction. Finally, Trent Rakins, Mid-Atlantic's Head of Client Services, broke the silence. He'd carefully cultivated both his take-charge demeanor and his 'success' image. His dark brown hair was expensively cut, and his charcoal-gray suit had been custom-tailored.

"Does anyone know when the funeral is going to be?"

Emma Yeats nodded and swallowed. "Ron's wife called an hour ago. It's Tuesday at eleven at the Ashlyn Country Club. It's just a memorial service. He wasn't religious."

"Is there going to be a viewing?"

Emma shook her head, her ink-black bob swinging as she crumpled a tissue in her hand. "No," she said.

"They don't want a big thing. But she – Mrs. Clemons – did say it would mean a lot if we're there. I'll email everyone the address."

"Thanks Emma," said Wade Messner, Mid-Atlantic's Head of Vendor Accounts. "I know this is hard for you." He reached out to pat her hand but then, remembering the company's sexual harassment training session from six months ago, thought better of it and put his own awkwardly back in his lap. He looked down at the page of notes in front of him.

After a silent moment or two, Wade looked up. His light brown eyes were slightly distorted by the steel-rimmed glasses he wore, and his pale blue Oxford-cloth shirt looked slightly rumpled under his navy suit. He rubbed the back of his neck and said, "I know we're all miserable and, but we do need to cover a few things while we're together." Then he glanced once more at his notes. "We'll need to plan some sort of public statement."

"Thanks Wade," Trent said, barely glancing in that direction. "We'll worry about what to say publicly later." He looked confidently around the table, choosing to ignore the glare he'd gotten from Wade. "For now, let's talk about the proposal I sent around on Monday about the direction we ought to be taking in the next few months."

"I read that proposal, Trent," said Denise Bascomb. As Mid-Atlantic's top Client Representative, her sales record was gilt-edged. She was responsible for some of the most lucrative accounts the company handled. She certainly looked impressive today, in a silver Armani jacket and black pants, her platinum hair coiled into a knot at the back of her head.

"What did you think?" Trent asked, giving her a bonded and veneered smile.

"Honestly? I don't think it's the image we want to project." Denise looked steadily at Trent.

"I'm not sure what you mean, Denise."

"You're proposing that we go after a completely different kind of client – not the kind we've handled before."

"And what's the problem with building our client base?"

"I'm all for building our base, Trent, you know that. But this proposal – well, it looks like you want us to start, well, a lot further down on the ladder." Denise looked a little embarrassed at the elitist implications of what she'd just said. "You know what I mean," she tried to recover herself. "We're used to dealing with pretty exclusive clients."

"I know,' Trent said. "They've been our bread and butter. But we have to diversify if we're going to stay competitive. That's what Ron…"

"What Ron what?" Emma looked up sharply. She wasn't usually one to speak up very often at meetings. But she'd been loyal to her boss. If Trent was about to bad-mouth Ron, there was no way she was going to sit and say nothing.

"Never mind, Emma," Trent said. "It's just that Ron could be a stick-in-the-mud about some things, that's all."

"About what?" Denise asked icily.

"I've been wanting to expand us into different markets for a while now. There are lots of opportunities out there that we're not grabbing. I told Ron, too. I told him we needed to change our focus."

"But we've always worked with top-of-the-market kinds of clients," Wade said. "I'm wondering what'll happen to our image if we change. Quite honestly, I think a change like that could dilute our brand."

"Wade, how about you do your job working with our vendors and let us handle this?" Trent snapped.

"How about you stop acting like a schoolyard bully!" Denise glared at Trent.

"Look, can we all just calm down for minute?" This came from Greg Isaacson, Head of Accounting and Payroll. He was usually soft-spoken and in general, came to these meetings more to provide reports than to help map out company strategy. So everyone stopped for a minute and looked at him. "I know I'm a number cruncher who doesn't usually deal with the clients. But I don't think this is the time to talk about this issue. Hell, Ron's not even in the ground yet! We have our business plan for the next six months anyway, so let's just stay with it, at least for now." He shook back his medium-length taffy-colored hair as he raised his head up to make his point.

There was an embarrassed silence as the others realized they'd been bickering like children.

"Greg's right," Trent conceded at last. "I still think we need to go in a different direction, but we can talk about it at our next meeting."

There were nods of agreement as the others picked up their notes. Slowly they filed out of the conference room, murmuring as they went. Emma was the last to leave since it was her responsibility to make sure that everything was secured. She glanced around the room to see if anything had been left behind and headed for the door to lock it after she went out. As she got there, she heard Greg say, "That wasn't a smart move, Denise, to bait him like that."

"Who, Trent? He's going to be history as soon as I step up."

"I just don't think you ought to be that obvious is all."

"Don't worry about me, Greg. Look, I have a client meeting in twenty minutes." Then, in a more hushed voice, "Come over later? About nine?"

Emma could barely hear Greg's reply. "I'll be there."

Two

Patricia Stanley's alarm dragged her out of a comfortable dream at five-thirty the next morning. Damnit, the alarm would wake Becky, and she didn't have to get up for another hour. Patricia flopped back down after turning it off and peered through half-closed eyes at the pillow next to her. Becky stirred a little, rolled over and murmured, "I get the whole blanket now."

"Yeah, you do. For now. Go back to sleep." Patricia gave Becky a quick hug, slipped out of bed and padded toward the bathroom. She hated waking her partner up early. Becky Lowry had a demanding job as a lab assistant at DynaGen Laboratories, a medical and forensic testing lab, so she treasured every moment of sleep she got. Well, there was nothing Patricia could do about it. She'd drawn early duty this week and she had to be at the station by seven. Hopefully Becky would be able to get back to sleep.

After she'd showered and brushed her teeth, Patricia put on the black jeans and lavender pullover that she'd hung on the back of the bathroom door. At least she'd thought to hang them there so she wouldn't have to grope her way through the darkened bedroom to look for them. A quick glance in the bathroom mirror, a little eyeliner and a ponytail for her damp hair and she was ready to go.

Traffic wasn't too bad, so there was time to stop for coffee and a large box of blueberry muffins on the way to work. There wasn't a set rule, but Patricia had learned that people informally took turns bringing in breakfast for the people who'd gotten morning duty. Today it was her turn. She pulled into the station's staff-only parking lot and got out of the car, placing the muffin box and coffee on the roof while she locked up. Then she picked up the breakfast things and went into the station. It was still a little bit of a thrill for her to actually be going into the station by the staff entrance, and not in uniform.

When she'd checked in, she put the muffins and coffee on the large counter and headed into the bullpen. "Coffee and muffins in the break room!" she called out as she sat down at her desk. She'd just turned on her computer when a sound made her look up. Luke had dropped his jacket over the back of his own chair.

"Morning," she said.

"Did I hear you say something about coffee when I walked in?"

Wordlessly, Patricia pointed towards the break room and began to look through her work email. Nothing of real interest. A few minutes later Luke returned, put his coffee on his desk and sat down.

"We get anything?" he asked.

"Not yet – not that I know of."

"Not so fast." Patricia and Luke both looked up at the sound of their boss Sergeant Ian Grant's voice. He was standing between their desks with a muffin in one hand and a piece of paper in the other. Once he had their attention, Grant went on. "I got a call from the Coroner's Office. They got a pathology report about that case you two had the other day - Ronald Clemons. Looks like something's going on with that death, and I want you to follow up. See

what they have to say and let me know what you
find out."
"Got it," Patricia said. Grant nodded and dropped
the piece of paper on her desk.
"While you do that," Luke said, "I'll call up what
we've already got on the guy."
"Thanks," Patricia said as she picked up her
telephone.

When she got through to the Coroner's Office, she
was connected with Kathryn Le Monte, who was
handling the case. After she explained why she was
calling, Kathryn said, "Just a minute while I call up
the file." A moment later, she was back on the line.
"OK, here it is. Ronald Clemons. The hospital
always does a few extra tests in heart cases like
these – cases where the patient wasn't in a high-risk
category." She studied Ronald Clemons' chart on
her computer screen as she went on. "And this time,
they found some things that indicate a high level of
digitoxin."
"Digitoxin? That's related to digitalis isn't it?"
Patricia asked as she scribbled in her notebook.
"That's right, Officer. In certain doses, some forms
of it used to be used for heart conditions, but it
hasn't been prescribed in a long time. And
especially not for basically healthy patients. So they
sent it over to us and we're assuming the medical
investigation."
"How much digitoxin did you find?"
"We've sent samples to the lab we use for further
testing. They're not back yet, so I can't give you
really detailed information. But I can tell you that
this death is unusual. We'll be looking into it from
our end, and we'll send whatever we've got to you
as soon as we can."

[27]

"Thanks."

Luke looked over as Patricia hung up the phone and raised his eyebrows expectantly. "Looks like we have something for Grant," she said. "That was Kathryn Le Monte over at the Coroner's Office. She said they found some high levels of digitoxin in our guy's system. Not something you normally see, and they're treating it as an unexpected death. They're going to do a medical investigation."
"Let's go brighten the boss' day."

Grant was on the phone when they got to his desk, but he gestured for them to come over and waved them to seats. When he'd finished his conversation, he said, "You have something for me?"
"Yeah," Patricia said. "The Coroner's Office says that Ronald Clemons had a high level of digitoxin in his system."
"They say whether they're treating it as suspicious?"
"Not in so many words,' Luke said. "But they're doing an investigation."
"All right. Let's not get ahead of ourselves. Let them do their tests. Stanley, go talk to the widow. Right now, we're just covering our asses, but it might prove helpful. Find out whether this guy was on any medication. Find out what his mental state was, too, if you can. Enders, I want you to do some background on this guy. Where he worked, that kind of thing. Let's find out what we can and see where it gets us.'
He looked at them both, said "Thanks" in a way that was clearly a dismissal, and turned towards his computer.

"I guess we get started," Luke said as they went back to their own desks.

"Yup," Patricia agreed.

Twenty minutes later, Patricia pulled out of the station parking lot in one of the standard police-issue cruisers. Her hands gripped the steering wheel a little too tightly as she joined the traffic. What the hell was she supposed to say to this woman? What do you say to someone who's just lost a husband? More than anything, she didn't want to come across as stupid or unprofessional, but she couldn't think of anything to say that wasn't either one or the other.

It didn't take very long to get to the Clemons' home. It was one of the nice ones off North Valley Road, with a decently-kept lawn and trees just waiting to sprout new leaves. As soon as the weather warmed up a little more reliably, the trees would probably look beautiful. Patricia pulled the cruiser into the driveway and zipped up her jacket as she got out. A cold knot formed in her stomach as she tried to figure out what she was going to say to Mrs. Clemons. She'd never done this on her own before. She'd always been with someone else – someone who did the actual talking. Well, she was the one doing it now. I hope to God I don't do something stupid, she thought as she approached the front door.

The sound of the doorbell echoed through the house as Rachel looked up from the books she was sorting. She hadn't been able to get to sleep the

night before, so at two o'clock she'd given up trying
and gone into Ron's study to go through some
things. She could still feel him in there – could
almost smell his after-shave. It was a good thing
Lina hadn't spent the night this time; Rachel wanted
to be alone right now. Sit quietly. Whoever it is will
go away. Then the doorbell rang again. Rachel
peeked out the study window to see who it was.
From her angle she could just see the edge of a car
with what looked like police markings. She couldn't
ignore a police visit – they would just come back.
Unwillingly, she straightened up from where she'd
been sitting on the floor, brushed off the back of her
tan slacks and slowly made her way downstairs.

By the time the bell rang for the third time Rachel
had gotten to the door and opened it. A young
woman with a blonde ponytail and a police-issue
jacket stood on the porch. "Yes?" she asked.
"Mrs. Clemons? I'm Officer Stanley." And she
showed Rachel an ID. "Can I come in for a
minute?"
It wouldn't be for 'a minute,' Rachel guessed. She
really wasn't ready for this, and it must have shown
on her face, because the woman said, "Please? I
promise it won't take long."
"All right." Rachel slowly opened the door and
gestured for the cop to come in.

Patricia looked around the living room she'd been
shown into as discreetly as she could. She was no
expert on furniture or decorating, but it looked very
tastefully put together to her. Charcoal gray sofa
and loveseat, pearl-gray carpet and cream-colored
walls.

"Please, have a seat," Mrs. Clemons (Please, call me Rachel) said.

"Thank you." Patricia sat down, not sure whether she ought to start the conversation.

"Can I get you anything? A cup of coffee?"

"Oh, no, thanks." Well, she couldn't sit staring like an idiot. "I'm – I'm very sorry for your loss, Ma'am."

"Thank you. It's been very difficult. Ron was a good person. What can I do for you?

The woman sounded almost like a robot, Patricia thought. Reciting all of the 'proper' polite things to say, but not really there. Well, who was she to say how people ought to grieve? She'd done it in her own way. "I'm sorry to bother you at a time like this. I know it must be terrible for you. Were you married a long time?" Awkward question! But she had to start somewhere. She wasn't going to learn anything if the woman wouldn't talk.

"Yes, twenty-five years."

Patricia saw the beginnings of a sad half-smile at the corners of Rachel's mouth as she went on. "We met – Ron and I – when we were competing for an advertising contract. We worked for rival companies at the time. He bet me dinner his company would get the contract. He lost and had to pay, but he was a good sport about it. We had a fun time, found we liked each other. We married a year and a half later."

"And are you still in the business?'

'I'm a graphics/web designer. You know – promo webs for companies. I have my own business here at home."

"Any children?" Another tough question. Who knew what it might trigger? But it was a fair one.

[31]

"We have a son, Jason. He lives in Boston. He works for a publisher there. He and his fiancée are getting married next year. Ron was so happy when he found out. Now he won't see the wedding" Rachel blinked hard and then swallowed. "But you didn't come here to talk about my son's wedding. And you've already offered your condolences. What can I do for you?"

"I'm wondering if you might be able to answer a few questions for me."

"Questions? Is there – is there a problem? I thought Ron had a heart attack. That's what they said at the hospital."

This was the hard part. "Yes, Ma'am. But the Coroner's Office is taking another look."

"Are you telling me it wasn't a heart attack?"

Be careful, Patricia told herself. Say nothing that could come back to you. "I'm sorry, Ma'am, I don't have the medical details. We're just trying to figure out what exactly happened."

"Well…I don't know how I can help you."

"We're really just trying to get a handle on how this happened. Was your husband taking any medication?"

"The doctors already asked me that."

"I know, Ma'am. Some of these questions might be repetitive. But it really will be helpful if you can answer them. It'll help us get a clear picture of things."

"He wasn't taking anything." Monotone voice again. Somewhat faraway, too, as though she weren't really talking to Patricia. "Nothing by prescription anyway. He took a painkiller if his back was hurting or he had a headache or something, like everybody else does. Nothing else."

"Do you know when the last time was that he had a medical examination?"

"I couldn't say for sure, but it was about eight months ago. Something like that. His doctor's office would have that information."

"We can ask them about that, then. Do you have a number for them?"

"I can find it."

"I'd appreciate that."

The sound of a car pulling into the driveway made both women look up. "Oh, I think that'll be my sister Lina. She's been helping out."

"I'm glad you have someone to be with you."

The back door opened and shut. Quick footsteps through what must be the kitchen. Then a tall woman with wavy auburn hair came into the room. Patricia could see the resemblance between the two women right away. "There you are,' the woman said as she walked in.

"Lina, this is Officer…"

"Stanley, Ma'am."

"Right, of course. I'm sorry. This is my sister, Lina Porter."

"Pleased to meet you," Patricia said.

"Is there some kind of problem, Officer?" Lina asked warily.

"We're just trying to get some details straight about Mr. Clemons' death, Ma'am."

"I'm not sure what you mean. Didn't he die of a heart attack?"

"We're just trying to fill in the blanks, that's all."

"Look, I know you're trying to do your job. But my sister's been through enough. She's burying her husband tomorrow. Maybe you could ask your questions another time?"

[33]

"I know it's a terrible time." Turning to Rachel, Patricia said, "We'll be in touch if there's anything else we need. And I am sorry for your loss." She nodded to both women and got up to leave.

"Oh, wait! That telephone number. I'll get it," Rachel said. She came back five minutes later holding a business card. 'Here it is."

"Thanks," Patricia said, tucking the card into her notebook. She left the room after once more thanking Rachel for her time.

On her way out to the car, Patricia could hear her footsteps echoing so loudly she was sure everyone in the county could hear them. A wave of nausea hit her as she slid into the car seat, but she managed to gulp it down. Focus, you idiot, she told herself. You're fine. God, that had been hard though. Grief – seeing it on people's faces –just tore you apart, especially if you'd been through it yourself. She hoped it would get easier with time. Blinking back a few instinctive tears, she got the car started and backed slowly out into the street.

Luke Enders had chosen a table in the corner of the café where he'd arranged to meet Patricia for lunch. He'd called her after his trip to Ronald Clemons' company to see how her morning had gone, and they'd agreed to catch up over coffee and sandwiches. It would be better to have everything organized and ready for the Sergeant when they got back to the station. He'd only been waiting about five minutes when he saw her walk in the door. Lifting his arm in a half-wave, he caught her eye, and in a moment or two she joined him at the table.

She pulled out one of the wooden chairs and sat down.

"Is it Ye Olde Country Day?" she asked softly as she looked around. The café had wooden floors, wooden beams, and walls decorated with 'country style' samplers and prints. There was even a cutesy copper kettle on the counter next to the cash register.

"Yeah, they do go for the rustic look here. But the food's pretty good."

For a moment they looked at their menus in silence. After her visit to Rachel Clemons, Patricia wasn't really hungry, but she knew she might not have time to eat again until that night. So when the waitress came to take their order, she chose a cup of chicken soup and a baguette. Luke ordered a roast beef sandwich platter – nothing wrong with his appetite.

"So, how'd it go?" he asked. "You sounded like hell on the phone."

"Yeah, it was hard." Patricia told him about her visit to the Clemons home. When she'd finished, Luke said, "I don't see where you did anything wrong."

"OK, maybe not wrong, but I felt awkward."

"I guess you get used to it."

"That's what I hope. Now, tell me what you found out."

Luke looked down at the notebook he'd been reviewing while he waited for Patricia. "Company's called Mid-Atlantic Publicity Services. It's a sort of boutique publicity outfit. Caters mostly to high-end clients. Classy operation, actually."

"Clemons owned this company?"

"I didn't have time to look into the legalities of it, but yeah, I think he did."

At that point the food arrived and the next few minutes were devoted to eating. After a few bites of her baguette, Patricia asked, "So what did you make of the place?"

Luke nodded as he swallowed a bite of his sandwich. "Seems like a well-organized place. I think there's a lot of tension there though."

"What do you mean?" Patricia was interested now.

"Lots of little remarks. You know, little digs at each other. Like when I asked their top salesperson about who might run things from now on, she said they might 'have to end up with' their second-in-command – his name is Rakins. She sure as hell wasn't happy about it."

"What happened when you talked to Rakins?"

"Said he was confident the company would move forward successfully. Some kind of corporate bullshit like that."

"You don't like him?"

"People with those fake bonded-teeth smiles annoy me. Can't help it." Luke grinned, and Patricia found herself grinning back. "You talk to anyone else?" she asked.

"Just Clemons' assistant Emma Yeats. She's all upset about the whole thing. Still, she was pretty helpful. Gave me lists of people Clemons met with the week before he died, staff meeting notes, that kind of thing."

Patricia had been watching Luke closely. "She pretty, Luke?"

"Who?"

"Who else? Emma Yeats."

"I didn't notice."

"Of course you did! I know you. You think she's cute."

[36]

"Screw you, Stanley!" Luke threw a paper napkin across the table at Patricia, who caught it neatly. They both laughed for a minute.

"OK, OK, let's forget about the beautiful Emma Yeats for now. You find out anything else we ought to tell Grant?"

"Not really. Nobody said anything awful about our guy. Maybe he took something by mistake. Or maybe he killed himself."

"Could be. But it didn't sound like he had any reason to kill himself. You didn't get the sense that the company was having problems, did you?"

"No, not unless they're hiding something. It didn't look like they were having any problems, but I didn't dig too deep. Not without Grant okaying it."

"I know what you mean. I didn't go too far either. But at the same time, it didn't sound like the wife hated him or anything. Well, we'll see what Grant says. Maybe there's more to it." Patricia glanced at her watch. "We'd better get back."

"Yeah, hopefully we'll catch Grant at his desk."

"See you back there." Patricia drew out enough money to pay for her half of the check, gave Luke a wave and headed back out to the police unit. Maybe Luke was right and she hadn't done anything stupid. Still, you never knew.

When Patricia got back to the station, she saw that Luke hadn't arrived yet. She was trying to decide whether to speak to Grant on her own or wait for her partner when Grant made up her mind for her. He must have seen her come in, because as soon as she sat down at her desk, he walked over to her and sat down in the olive-green folding chair between her desk and Luke's. His prematurely white hair and moustache made him look almost like a professor, but he was all cop.

"So how'd it go? Where are we on this Ronald Clemons death? I got a call from one of the local papers. The word's gotten out and they want a statement."

"I went to the house – nice place. The widow's name is Rachel Clemons. She's a graphics/web site designer. They have one son – lives in Boston. Anyway, she said he wasn't on any medication and hadn't been ill."

"What was his mood like lately? Did she say?"

Oh, *damn*! She'd forgotten to ask about that. What if it was suicide? Grant read her facial expression.

"You didn't ask about it, right?"

"Sorry." *Shit*! Nice one, Stanley!

"It's not easy to remember everything. Give her a call when we're done and find out. We need to know."

"I will."

"Anything else?"

"I didn't push it too far. We don't know what we're dealing with and I didn't want to alienate her. But I didn't get the feeling she hated him or wanted him dead. Actually, if anything, she seemed kind of out of it."

"Drugs?"

"No, I don't think so. Just, not really there. She's just lost her husband, so I got the feeling she's on auto-pilot."

Grant nodded. "Yeah, I can see that."

Patricia hesitated for a moment and then decided to go ahead with it. "Does this smell like a murder to you?"

Grant leaned back slightly and looked up at the ceiling. "Hard to say," he answered at last. "Nothing definite, unless Enders came up with something?"

"Not that I know of. He'll brief you when he gets in, but he didn't give me the impression he found anything."

"Right. Well, if he didn't, then it's not going to be easy. Still, the preliminary coroner's report says suspicious death. High levels of digitoxin and no heart condition. To me, that smells. Especially if you find out he wasn't suicidal."

The two of them were still talking when Luke walked in. "Hey, why didn't I get the party invitation?" he joked as he slid into his seat.

"Check your email next time,'" Patricia fired back.

"Good timing, Enders," Grant said. "How'd you do this morning?"

"Not much to report, really," Luke answered. "The guy's company seemed to be doing fine. No signs they were in trouble, although I didn't check their finances closely. Everybody had the usual things to say about Clemons. You know, 'Great guy! We'll miss him. Soul of the company. What'll we ever do without him?' That kind of stuff."

"Anybody seem like they were lying?"

"Not so it was obvious."

"All right. Not bad, both of you, for a morning's work. Let's move on to next steps. I'll get the OK for us to get Clemons' financial records. Then we'll talk to everyone again. See what we can find out. I'll go along for the ride this time." Neither Patricia nor Luke liked the feeling of being babysat, but a suspicious death was not the same thing as a routine set of questions about a sudden heart attack. Still, it rankled. Grant guessed it would and added, "Nothing to do with you either of you guys. Just covering our asses. We don't want to get caught with our pants down." He waited until he saw both of them nod, and then went on. "Anybody know when the funeral – or whatever they're doing – is?"

"Tomorrow," Luke and Patricia spoke at the same time.

"What time?"

"They told me eleven," Luke said. "It's going to be at the Ashlyn Country Club. Oh, and for what it's worth, they're doing a memorial service."

"I've heard of that place," Grant said as he wrote down the information. "OK, I think one of us ought to be there tomorrow."

I'll go," Patricia said. She didn't really want to, but it was important to show you were a team player.

Grant nodded his thanks and made more notes. "OK, Enders, while Stanley's at the memorial service, you can be starting with the financial angle. Before you leave today, find out where the company banked. Find out where he banked personally, too. We can go for full reports once I get the OK, but let's not waste too much time."

Luke made some notes as his boss was speaking. "OK, can either of you think of other questions we should be starting to ask?"

"Should we start working on the digitoxin thing?" Luke asked.

"Yeah, we'll need to do that. We'll need to find out if there's any way to get it locally."

"What about whether it's grown locally? Doesn't that come from foxglove?" Patricia asked.

"I think so. Might be a good idea to find out more about local plants." Grant nodded towards Patricia again. Good! Maybe she'd redeem herself for forgetting about the suicide question. Mental note – call the widow right away and find out about that. Grant looked at his watch and started to stand up. "I think we've all got busy afternoons. Let's get to it."

When he left, Patricia took a deep breath.
"Something wrong?" Luke asked.
"I screwed up – forgot to ask the widow whether there were any signs this might be a suicide. I'm not looking forward to talking to her again today. Especially since it was my fault."
"Don't feel bad," Luke reassured her. He looked up to be sure that Grant wasn't nearby. Then he leaned closer to Patricia and said, "I never even thought to ask at the company. Guess we'd better both get on the phone."

At five-thirty, Patricia hung up the telephone on her desk and took a deep breath. It had taken her two tries to get through to Rachel Clemons. The first time the line had been busy and the second time another voice (the sister's?) had said that Rachel was resting and couldn't talk. Finally, she'd managed to speak to the woman herself. It hadn't been a particularly enlightening conversation, though. Rachel insisted that her husband hadn't been moody or depressed lately ("He was concerned about work things, like always, but depressed? No."). He hadn't been taking any medication either ("You people have already asked me about that. Oh, I see. No, no anti-depressives.").

For a few minutes she sat, slightly slumped down in her chair, staring at the notes she'd made from her conversation and tapping a finger on her desk. It just didn't seem to be a suicide. And Luke had told her that nobody at the company suggested that Clemons had been suicidal either. But at the same time, Patricia'd heard nothing to suggest that this was an angry, vengeful widow. She truly seemed grief-stricken. "Same here," Luke said. "No obvious hatred at all." Maybe this was just a freakish natural death. It happened. But the Coroner's Office didn't think so.

"Earth to Stanley. Come in, Stanley." The voice behind her made Patricia jump a little.
"Where were you?" Grant asked.
"Just thinking about this," she gestured towards her notes. "No signs of suicide according to the widow."
"Did Enders find anything? And where the hell is he, anyway?"
"No, he didn't. The word at the company is that Clemons was fine. And Luke's on a vending machine run."
"All right. Just put together what you have and get it to me before you leave. Tell Enders, too."
"Got it."

Grant walked away, and Patricia went back to looking at her notes. A minute later a bag of potato chips sailed over her left shoulder and landed squarely on her lap. She picked the bag up. "Oh, yeah! Barbecue!"
"Ranch are the only ones that are worth eating," Luke retorted as he plunked a bottle of water on her desk. He dropped his own chips and water on his desk and sat down.

"Oh, before I forget. Grant wants us to write up what we've found on the Clemons case. He wants copies before we leave."

"Coming up."

"Luke, do you think there's anything to this whole thing?"

"Honestly? I've been wondering too. The boss thinks there might be, or he wouldn't have us working on it. There's enough to do around here without giving us busy work."

"Got that right," Patricia said, looking ruefully at the pile of papers on the corner of her desk.

"Who knows? Maybe you'll pick up something at the memorial service tomorrow."

Oh, God, the memorial service! Why had she agreed to do that? Idiot! Being a team player was fine, but funerals and memorial services were a lot for her to handle. "Yeah, maybe," she finally said. Luke took in her facial expression. "What? Did I say something?"

"No. It's fine. Just thinking of something, that's all."

Luke nodded and the two of them got to work on the reports that Grant had requested.

An hour later, Patricia pushed the 'Print' button on the write-up of her visit and telephone calls. She stretched hard, got up and walked across the room to the communal printer. Sifting through the papers in the tray, she picked out her report and brought it to Grant.

He grunted his thanks and then said, "Now get the hell out of here, Stanley, before I find something else for you to do."

He didn't need to tell her twice.

[43]

Ten minutes later she got into her old Honda and
headed for home. Home, some Chinese food, a
couple of beers. And Becky. Yup, that's what she
needed.

"You home?" she called out as she unlocked the
door to their apartment.
"Kitchen!" Becky called back. She'd just shut the
refrigerator door when Patricia walked in.
"Did I just see what I think I saw?"
"What, the Tsingtao?"
"Yes of course the Tsingtao! How could you
possibly have known I was in the mood for Chinese
and beer?"
"I'm psychic."
"No, you're just really good to me." Patricia gave
Becky a long hug.
"What's the matter, honey?"
'Long day, that's all.'
"C'mon, let's sit down, crack a beer and you can
tell me about it."

Patricia nodded and opened the refrigerator. She
grabbed two beers and followed Becky into the
small living room as the refrigerator door closed
behind her. Becky sat down on the beige-and-
chocolate-striped living room sofa and patted the
seat beside her. Patricia joined her, took a sip of
beer and put the bottle on the faux-oak coffee table
in front of the sofa.
"Now, talk," Becky said.
"OK, so we have this guy who suddenly dies.
Coroner's Office says it's an unusual death. They're
planning to classify it as suspicious, I think.
Anyway, the boss has me and Luke following up on

[44]

the case, which is fine. But I don't know if there's anything there."

Becky thought for a moment. "Why are they saying it's suspicious?"

"High levels of digitoxin in the system, and no pre-existing heart condition."

"That *is* weird. I don't think I've ever seen digitoxin in samples before. I mean, we learned about it, but I haven't seen it at the lab."

"Well, that's the thing. Something strange is going on, that's for sure."

Becky took a long look at Patricia's face and then said. "Out with it. There's more. I know you." Patricia felt tears pricking the back of her eyes as she looked back. "It's just that – well, I went to visit the widow. It was – it was really hard. I nearly puked, OK?"

"You'll get better at it."

"It's not just talking to the widow. It was everything. It reminded me of, well, of Serena. I'm sorry." Serena. Beautiful Serena. Musically gifted, loving, fun. But that was a few years ago. She ought to be able to handle it by now. You *are* getting better, you know, Dr. Zara had said. Give it time. Becky put her arm around Patricia and hugged her hard. "It's OK. You're allowed to miss her. She was a big part of your life."

"I know. But so are you."

"I'm not going anywhere. You'll be OK. We'll be OK."

"I'm trying. I just keep thinking how it was when Serena was killed. And the whole poison thing just brings it all back again. I'm sorry."

"There's nothing to be sorry for."

"How the hell do you put up with me?"

"Um – like I have no faults?"

"Well," Patricia said, wiping her eyes with the back of her hand, "You do steal my pillow all the time." She managed a weak smile.

"There you go! Now, you sit here and finish that beer. I'm going down the street to pick up our dinner. I'll be right back."

"I'll be here."

Becky gave Patricia's leg a swift pat, got up and headed towards the door, picking up her purse as she went. Patricia watched her leave and then leaned back against the sofa and closed her eyes. Thank God for Becky, she thought.

Three

The Ashlyn Country Club wasn't a long drive from Paoli, but Patricia had never been there before, so she allowed plenty of time to get there. You can do this, you can do this, you can do this, she reminded herself. You won't fall apart, you'll be fine. Nothing to worry about. She idly punched buttons for the different radio stations she'd programmed into her stereo, but nothing calmed her. Finally, she turned the radio off in disgust. Nothing but ads and loud-mouthed 'radio personalities' anyway. Not long now. You can do this. You can do this.

The entrance to the country club was a wide semi-circle of drive that passed the club's main entrance and went on to end in a large parking area. Patricia found a spot, parked her Honda and took a deep breath. She glanced down at her black skirt and black-and-gray patterned silk blouse. At least her clothes were right. She got out of the car and walked slowly towards the club's entrance, head down against the chilly wind that had sprung up while she was driving. A few people were standing near the double glass doors at the entrance, but the wind discouraged a lot of outdoor conversation. Patricia didn't know anyone anyway, so she went straight in.

Just inside the doors was a lobby area with navy and hunter green patterned carpet and several round teakwood tables. Each table had four teakwood armchairs with navy upholstery. On each table was a vase of dark purple hyacinths with a black ribbon around it. A few people were standing in small

[47]

groups, but Patricia hadn't yet seen Rachel or her sister – Lina, that was it. Lina Porter. Maybe they were in the ladies' room. A few feet into the lobby was a small sign on a stand. In black calligraphy, the sign directed people to the memorial service, which would take place down the hall in the Rosewood Room. Patricia glanced at her watch – five minutes to eleven. Time to go in.

Inside the Rosewood Room, everything was ready for the service. There was a small podium in front of the room, and dozens of chairs had been arranged to face it. At least the chairs looked comfortable, with dark red cushions on the seats and backs. Patricia chose one towards the back of the room and began to look around at the rest of the people. Rachel was close to the front, with Lina next to her. Next to Lina was a tall man with dark thinning hair and a small goatee – must be her husband. On Rachel's other side was a young man who looked a lot like the victim. That would be the son, Jason.

They talked in low voices as other people started to file into the room. A few people went up to the family to pay their respects; others took their seats. Patricia watched the family carefully. How cold is this, she thought. I'm looking at these grieving people and wondering if any of them is a murderer. It was hard to step back like that, but it kept her from thinking too much, and that helped. It certainly didn't look as though there was a lot of discord. The four of them sat down in a row and Patricia could see occasional glances and shoulder squeezes. They really did look like they were trying to get each other through this. Still, you never knew.

Rachel glanced around and behind her now and again. There were the people from Ron's office. Good. Emma had said they'd all be coming. In another small group were some of Ron's poker buddies. Rachel's eyes filled up for the fifteenth time that day as she thought about Ron's sacred Friday night poker game. She hadn't even minded when it was their turn to host. There were other people too that Rachel recognized. Some friends from the club, some of her work clients, and a few acquaintances. Wait, who was that in the back? Oh, yes, that cop. The one who had come over the other day. She looked so different in dress clothes and makeup. She hadn't known Ron – what was she doing here?

Just then the funeral director stepped to the microphone and cleared his throat discreetly. Everyone quieted down and turned towards the podium. After the introduction, Reverend Warren began. Thank you for coming we all miss Ron so much this is a sad day for everyone but let us remember that... Rachel lost track of his words. He wasn't even talking about the Ron she knew. Not the man Ron, just some cardboard cutout person with Ron's name. Not a real person. But then, none of this felt real anyway. Rachel looked over at Jason. He stared steadily ahead, not a muscle in his face moving. Her eyes dropped as she thought about how hard it must be for him. He'd barely spoken to her since he got in last night. Hopefully they'd get a chance to talk later.

Reverend Warren was finishing up. And so, let's try not to focus on our grief but instead focus on the

good years we had with Ron. Let's remember what
an important part of our lives he was. Rachel tried
to pay attention, but it made no sense. Try not to
focus on our grief? What else was there to focus on?
Ron was gone. Dead. Dead. What are we supposed
to do, forget that everything is empty now?

The minister ended his sermon by inviting Rachel
up to 'say a few words.' Why did they always call it
that? 'A few words.' "Go on, honey," Lina
whispered. "You can do it."
Rachel nodded and slowly walked to the podium.
When she got there, she put down the piece of paper
where she'd written her notes. She looked around,
not really seeing anyone. "Thank you for coming.
Ron was the most important…"

"…part of my life for more than twenty-five
years…." Patricia watched as Rachel gave her
speech. She didn't even seem quite human, more
like a robot. Monotone voice, staring straight ahead,
looking utterly vulnerable in her black suit and
black flat shoes. She seemed so small up there
although she was actually of average height. It was
as though she had shrunk into herself. "…and so I
would like to conclude by saying how much Ron
cared about all of you. He was that kind of man."
Rachel made her way almost blindly back to her
seat, where her sister took her hand.

A few other people came up and gave short
speeches. He was a fine colleague, a hard worker,
cared about clients, always dependable, ethical, all
the rest of it. People said those kinds of things at
memorial services and funerals, but these people

really seemed to mean it. Luke had said that none of the people he talked to had seemed to hate Ron Clemons. But people lied. And people didn't know each other as well as they thought they did.

After the speeches were over, the minister thanked everyone for coming and announced refreshments in the lobby. Patricia didn't feel hungry at all. More than anything, she wanted to get out of there. But it would be a good chance to see how everyone interacted and besides, she was never going to be good at her job if she couldn't get past personal things. So, she made her way slowly towards the group of people who were waiting to speak to Rachel and her family. When it was her turn, Patricia shook hands first with Rachel, who thanked her mechanically. Then Rachel said, "This is my son, Jason. Next to him is my sister Lina – but you've met Lina – and her husband Kyle." Patricia moved along to shake Jason's hand. He stared straight ahead and only nodded when she spoke to him. Lina seemed more together, but tense. At least she made eye contact though. Kyle Porter seemed quiet, but pleasant enough.

Finally, Patricia got to the door into the lobby. A bar had been set up along one side of it, and a few people were already sipping glasses of wine. Buffet tables lined the other walls – apparently no expense spared on the food. The thought of eating made her feel a little sick, so she went over to the bar instead and asked for a club soda. Not her usual choice, but it would hopefully settle her stomach. Then she found a chair in a quiet corner of the room and took a seat. As soon as she finished her club soda and got herself together, she'd leave.

"You have to eat something," Lina urged as she guided Rachel to a table. "You want me to get you a plate?"

"No, really," Rachel answered. "I don't want anything. Maybe later. Right now, I just want to sit."

Jason sat next to her, still saying nothing. She looked over at him as Lina and Kyle went to get food. "You OK?" she asked quietly.

"OK? No, I'm not OK!" he snapped. Then he looked away and back again. He saw her facial expression and said, "I'm sorry, Mom, I'm sorry. I didn't mean – it's just that..."

"I know. Me, too." So like his father. Ron's dark brown wavy hair and hazel eyes, but her chin and jaw line. Still, he had a lot of his father's mannerisms - or was she just looking for that? Sometimes it was almost like looking at a younger Ron. She wouldn't say that, though. Jason had to be his own person.

"You want anything?" Jason finally asked, trying to make amends.

"Some water?"

"Sure." Jason got up, probably glad for something to do, and headed towards the bar.

When he'd gone, Rachel looked around the room. So many faces – too many. The noise of the conversation was getting to her and things people said to her kept fading in and out. I'm so sorry, Ron was a great person, is there anything I can do, do you need anything, would you like me to stop by? And always with a slight look of relief when she reassured them she'd be OK. Nobody liked to be around a grieving person – it was too hard. Once they'd done their duty, people were happy to gather in small groups and talk to each other. Just as well really; she didn't have anything to say to them anyway.

After a moment she noticed Officer Stanley in one of the corners, drinking what looked like a soft drink. What was she still doing there? She hadn't known Ron. She'd asked about Ron's medications and suicide too, saying it was 'routine paperwork.' But coming to the memorial service? That wasn't routine, was it? Rachel had already asked if there was something wrong about Ron's death, and Officer Stanley hadn't answered. Whatever was going on, it wasn't right for her to be here. This was for people Ron knew. Just her presence reminded Rachel that Ron hadn't died peacefully, in his sleep, the way you always see it in obituaries. It was like a long cold shadow that you stayed away from if you could.

"Honey, what is it?" Lina asked when she and Kyle returned.
"It's just – oh, thanks, Jason," she said as her son came up, handed her a water with lemon, and sat down.
"You weren't done. What is it?" Lina persisted.
"I'm just being crazy, that's all. I just – well, I want to get out of here."
"I know it's been hell for you – and you," Lina included both Rachel and Jason in her glance.
"This'll end in an hour and then we can all go home and rest."

Rest, that's what she needed. Just silence and rest. For a long, long, time. She looked across the room for Officer Stanley again, but she'd gone.

Patricia sat in her car for a few minutes with her eyes closed, breathing the chilly damp air. She was glad to have a few minutes alone, and even more glad to be away from the hot, stuffy room filled with food smells. Once she could think clearly again, she went back over what she'd seen and heard. No evidence of friction in the family. No signs of bitterness, gloating, or backbiting among the work colleagues either. She hadn't talked to any of the other guests, really. It sure as hell wasn't a time for interviews and to be honest, not a time for arguments or discord either. Even beneath the veneer of good manners, though, it had seemed that Ronald Clemons was well-liked. Still, there were those weird lab findings, and the Coroner's Office wouldn't likely get interested in a case if there was no reason. So maybe somebody had killed the victim. But if that person had been at the service, he or she was a good actor.

That was enough thinking about it all for one day. It would probably be better anyway to put it out of her mind and dive into the dozens of other things that were probably waiting for her back at the station. She took a deep breath, put her car in gear and prepared to leave.

As she did so she glanced into her rearview mirror. She could see a few people leaving the club, and two of them seemed to have gotten into an argument. Who were they again? They'd both given short speeches at the memorial service, but she couldn't remember their names. They both worked at Mid-Atlantic though; that much she remembered. A woman with platinum hair and a guy with dark brown hair. Both dressed to kill and both looking as though they'd like to. She'd have to ask Luke about them when she got back to the station. Maybe it had nothing to do with Ronald Clemons' death. But she'd look pretty stupid if it did and she didn't mention it. If this was a murder, she wanted to be kept on it, and that wouldn't happen if she didn't cover all the bases. After a quick check to be sure nobody was looking her way, she pulled her telephone out and took a picture of the couple, just in case it would be useful.

"Well, you didn't have to mention it here of all places!" Trent snapped. "Couldn't this have waited until we got back to the office?"

"All I said was that we need to talk about where we're going to go from here, that's all. There's no crime in that," said Denise. Trent looked behind him and saw that other people were also coming out of the club. He steered Denise to a grassy spot away from the door, so they wouldn't be overheard.

"He's not even in the ground yet and you're already planning the company's future?"

"Oh, stop being so goddamned high and mighty, Trent! You're the one who wants to change everything."

"I'm not bringing it up at the memorial service, though. At least I have some tact."

"I know you, though, Trent. As soon as we get back to the office, you'll hole yourself up in your office and later announce all sorts of major changes without even consulting us. I figured I'd get in there while I had the chance."

"Look, I've got to get back to the office. I'll talk to you when you've calmed down."

Trent glared at Denise and strode towards his Lincoln. Denise watched him go for a moment and then headed towards her own Mercedes. Calm down? He wanted her to calm down? He'd find out how calm she could be. He wasn't going to get away with condescending to her like that, that was for sure. She got into her car and looked angrily around, silently daring anyone to try to pull out of the parking lot in front of her.

An hour later the last guest shook Rachel's hand and left. Staff members were removing the food dishes and cleaning the tables, and the bartenders were closing down their operation. Rachel sat down silently and rubbed her forehead. Lina sat down next to her.

"We made it," she said.

"This just doesn't seem real," Rachel said quietly. "It's like I'm watching this film or something."

"You'll be OK. C'mon, let's find Jason and Kyle and get out of here." Rachel nodded and looked around. Nobody there but the staff, quietly cleaning up. It was almost peaceful.

"I just want to sit for a few minutes," she said. "It's quiet now."

"You stay here, then, and I'll go look for the guys. Back in a minute." Lina got up in that brisk way of hers and went down the hall. Rachel breathed in and out for a few minutes. Sitting and breathing. Yes, that was enough for now.

A few minutes later Jason joined her. "Ready?" he asked.

"Where are your aunt and uncle?"

"Uncle Kyle's in the bathroom. Aunt Lina's waiting for him."

"All right. Guess we'd better go." Rachel got to her feet and gave her son's arm a squeeze.

"I don't have to go back to Boston in the morning," he suddenly said.

"Jason, you've got your job, you've got Felicia, you've got enough on your plate. You don't have to stay and babysit me. I'll be fine."

"I know, Mom. I want to. I can always call Felicia, and I've got two more days of bereavement leave time coming to me if I want it."

"Let's not argue about it now. I just don't want you to feel you have to stay."

Just then, Lina and Kyle came from the direction of the restrooms. "You want us to come back with you?" Lina asked.

"No, you don't need to," Rachel said. "Jason's staying the night and besides, right now I just want some time to myself."

"Are you sure? I don't know if that's a good idea."

"Lina, I'm fine, OK? Really."

"If you say so," Lina said with an edge in her voice. "I'm just trying to help."

"I know you are. And I'm grateful. I don't know what I would have done without you these last few days. But I'll be OK."

Slightly mollified, Lina turned to Kyle and said, "You want to drive, or should I?"

"I will."

She turned towards Rachel as they left. "I'll call you later," she promised.

When Kyle and Lina had left, Rachel said, "Guess it's our turn now." She and Jason walked silently out to the silver Prius Ron had gotten her as a birthday gift last year. Now she handed the keys to Jason. So much like Ron as he got into the car and got ready to drive. Don't think about it. Jason is Jason. "You want to stop anywhere along the way?" he asked.

"No, thanks. I just want to go home and have a drink and sit for a long time."

"A drink sounds good to me, too. You think Aunt Lina'll come over?"

"I told her she didn't need to."

"I know. You think she will anyway?"

"She means well, Jason."

"I know she does. But sometimes she's like – she's like a heavy blanket that you can't kick off when you get too warm."

Amen to that, Rachel thought. She didn't want to bad-mouth her sister in front of Jason. And Lina had been wonderful lately. But Jason had a point. Just like the kind of thing Ron would have said. Ron joking about Lina. Ron asking when she was going to start clucking.

"Mom, you OK?"

"Sorry, a million miles away."

It was five-thirty the next morning. Rachel lay in bed looking out the window at the darkness outside.

She'd always liked the feeling of freedom you got when you looked out a window. It was still too cold to leave the windows open at night, but it wouldn't be long before she'd be able to smell the morning air and hear the first bird calls when she woke up. But right now, it was quiet. The quiet had a sound of its own when you thought about it. It could be oppressive, or it could be peaceful; it was all in how you looked at it.

She slowly turned over and crawled out from under the maroon-and-navy diamond pattern quilt. She'd never liked the look of it much, but Ron had thought it was great. And it was warm and comfortable. Down the hall to the bathroom and then to the kitchen to make coffee.

She'd just put the coffee pot on when she heard the soft thud of the paper landing against the front door. She crossed to the landing, went downstairs to the front door and looked out the peephole. Then she opened the door, got the paper and went back inside, locking the door behind her. It was chilly out on the front porch, but the smell of spring was there. It wouldn't be long.

A few minutes later she sat staring at the front page, sipping her coffee. There was nothing about Ron's memorial service in the paper. But then, why would there be? The rest of the world had just gone on as usual. It was odd, really. A small part of her had expected the news to be all over the front page. She was still looking at the headlines fifteen minutes later when Jason came in wearing a t-shirt and a pair of track pants.

"You're up early," she said.

"Yeah, I want to go for a run before I pack."

"You're lucky. It's a clear morning."

"Good," he said, pouring himself a cup of coffee. He sat down next to her, put his cup down and said, "Mom, can I ask you something?"

"Sure," she said, closing the newspaper.

"It's about Dad."

"OK," she said more slowly. She wasn't sure she was ready for this kind of conversation yet, but Jason wouldn't be here for long. She didn't want to shut him off if he wanted to talk. He'd said so little since he got here that she hardly had any idea what he was thinking. Now might be her chance to find out.

"How did he die?" Jason looked steadily at her. It was almost unnerving.

"You know that. He had a massive heart attack. Honey, I told you all of this."

"I know. I don't mean the heart attack part. I mean what caused it?"

"I don't know exactly. I'm not an expert."

"Didn't they tell you?"

"They didn't have the full report yet. They said it can take some time."

"That means there's something wrong, doesn't it?"

"Jason, where is this all coming from?"

He took a sip of his coffee but didn't say anything for a moment. But his face hardened, as though he'd made up his mind about something. "Ever since you called, I haven't been able to stop thinking about it. I mean, here Dad is. He's not old, he's pretty healthy, he's not even overweight, he's never had heart trouble, and he dies from a heart attack? It makes no sense at all. Don't you wonder?"

"Look, I'm doing well just to wake up and get through the day at this point. I'm not thinking about that, no. I'm putting one foot in front of the other. That's all I can do right now."

"Mom, I'm sorry. I know this is awful for me. I can't imagine what it's like for you. But he was my Dad. If something's wrong, I want to know."

"I can't answer you. Not right now."

"Mom, what if someone killed him?"

"Killed your dad?" Her coffee was cold and forgotten now. All she could see were Ron's eyes looking at her from her son's face. Say something, say something, say anything. "Why would anyone kill your dad?"

"I don't know. I don't even know why I'm saying that. It's just that the 'sudden heart attack' thing doesn't fit."

"Don't you think it could be that you just want answers? You want this all to make sense. Hell, so do I. I don't blame you. But some things don't make sense. They just happen."

"Getting hit by a car can just happen. But this kind of thing doesn't just happen."

For a few minutes neither one said anything. Then Jason absently stirred his coffee and said, "Do you think it was suicide? I haven't been around much. Maybe something was wrong. Was he upset?"

"The police asked me that, too," Rachel said with a slight sound that might have been a laugh. "I told them he'd been fine. And I'm telling you the same thing."

"So, if he didn't kill himself and if his heart was normal, then someone killed him. You see where I'm coming from?"

"I do see. But I also see that you're upset. I'm upset. We're not thinking straight."

Jason looked down at his coffee again and then up at his mother. "Yeah, that's probably what it is. I'm going running now. Be back in a little while." He got up, squeezed his mother's shoulder and left the kitchen. She heard the bang of the door as he left. Then there was quiet again.

Jason was a strong-minded young man. No, let's face it – stubborn. He'd always been that way. Once he got an idea, he wouldn't let go of it. Rachel remembered how he'd taught himself to play the guitar. He'd found an old guitar on one of the 'for sale' web sites and brought it home. "But you can't play," she'd said. "I'll learn," was his answer. And he had. It had taken weeks and plenty of calluses on his fingers, but he'd taught himself. And now he thought his father had been…

"…murdered." Sergeant Grant said. "That's the official word, and we've got the go-ahead to investigate. I just heard this morning. I'm going to be leading the team since we already know this case, and I want you two on it."

"I'm there," Luke said quickly.

Patricia shifted a little in her chair and looked up at Grant, who'd taken his usual seat between her desk and Luke's. "Count on me," she said, before he could change his mind. A chance to be on a murder investigation. That was something she'd wanted for the past couple of years, since she'd finished her police academy training. Let's be honest, she told herself, it's what nearly every cop wants – the chance to get the bad guys. She and Serena had talked a lot about that during those two o'clock-in-the-morning conversations people have at college. They would sit in the dormitory lounge, wrapped in blankets, drinking hot cocoa and sometimes wine, planning their futures. Serena had always said Patricia would a great cop. But then Patricia had seen what real murder was like. Serena's death had changed everything. And the investigation had been terrible for everyone – nothing like a TV cop show. Besides, she'd only been on the force for a few years. God knows what kind of mistakes she'd make.

Something in her face must have given her away, because Grant said, "This is your first homicide, isn't it, Stanley?"
"Yeah, 'fraid so."
"Yours too, Enders?"
"Yeah." Luke looked down at his desk.
"Nothing to be ashamed about. Everybody's got a first time. You two'll be fine or I wouldn't have put you on the team. Besides, with one of my people out with the 'flu, and another one on paid leave, I need you both. But there's a few things we're going to get clear now. First: neither of you is to even think about playing hero. We work together on this case. That means we share everything we get. You do *not* go out chasing anything on your own."
Luke and Patricia nodded and then Grant went on.
"Second: I'll sit in on all your interviews, at least at first. I know you've already talked to some of these people. I also know you're good cops. You wouldn't be on this case if you weren't. But you're new to murder cases and ultimately, I have to answer for everything we do. So, don't take it personally."

[63]

"Got it," Luke said. Patricia nodded her agreement. "Good. Now we got that out of the way, let's get started."

For the next half-hour, the three of them compared notes on the information they had, the people they'd already spoken to and the impressions they'd gotten. Nothing jumped out as an obvious lead but as Grant reminded them, they were just getting started. Finally, he said, "OK, I think we've done what we can do for the moment. Enders, I want you to find out who the guy's lawyer is. When you do, try to get us in there this afternoon. We'll see if there's anything in the will we should be looking at. Stanley, start the warrant paperwork, so we can see if we can get his phone records. Maybe there's something there. Let me know what you find out and we'll go from there. We'll want his appointment records, too." Grant went back to his desk and Patricia and Luke got busy with the telephones.

Within an hour Luke had managed to get through to Clemons' lawyer, Christine Kramer, who could see them at two o'clock. Patricia was transferred three times before she got to speak to the right person at Clemons' phone service provider. When she'd finally been connected, she explained why she was calling. Yes, they could verify that Ronald Clemons was a customer. Yes, they'd be happy to co-operate once they had a warrant.

Patricia was still annoyed as she hung up the phone. She didn't like the idea of just anyone being able to get anyone else's phone records, but at the same time, it was annoying to have to jump through all of the hoops sometimes. And anyway, it was nearly time for lunch. She looked across at Luke, who was talking on the phone. When he finished his call, she asked him, "You taking a lunch break?"

"Yeah, I didn't get time for breakfast this morning."

"Deli or pizza?"

"Deli. We going out or ordering in?"

"Out."

"Sounds good. We better see if the boss wants anything." They checked with Grant, who said he'd brought his lunch. Then they went out to the car they'd been issued for the day. Patricia would rather have walked, but there was nothing nearby. Oh, well, a change of scenery wouldn't hurt them.

The afternoon was almost as frustrating for Patricia as the morning had been. Luke and Grant were going to see the lawyer, something Patricia had wanted to do. But as the boss had said, it might be intimidating to have three cops on one interview. And besides it wasn't a good use of time.

"I want you to get our victim's background, Stanley. Motor vehicle history, criminal history if there is one, any public records, anything you can get. I want to know where this guy has lived, if he's ever been married before, the whole thing." Grant took one look at Patricia's face and added, "It's not busy work. We need all of it."

The fact that he was right about that didn't make it much better. Luke gave her an apologetic shrug as he followed the boss out of the station.

The law office of Tinport, Danvers and Streitzmann was one of the better-established and more reputable firms in the area. They mostly dealt with business law, but a few of the attorneys handled some private clients too. When Luke and Grant got to the building, they were shown into a small conference room with peach colored walls, chocolate-and-peach carpet and mahogany table and chairs. Within a few minutes Christine Kramer had joined them. She was short, with tight gray curls and a courteous but guarded manner.

"So," she said after introductions had been made. "I understand you're here about our client, Ronald Clemson. Is that right?"

Grant nodded subtly to Luke, who said, "Yes, that's correct. We're investigating his death and we have a few questions."

"I understood he died of a heart attack. Isn't that so?"

"At this stage we're just gathering information, and we'd really appreciate your help."

Recognizing that she wasn't going to get much more out of them, the attorney said carefully, "I'll certainly try to help."

"Thank you. When was the last time you had contact with Mr. Clemons?" Luke asked.

She looked at the day-planer she'd brought with her. "It was three months ago. He came in to review his will."

"Did he make any changes in it?"

"To tell you the truth, I'm a little uncomfortable discussing even a deceased client's personal business. But I understand why you're asking. No, he did not change the terms of his will."

"What were those terms?"

She sighed a little and then said. "Please understand that this is confidential." Both men agreed. "All right, then, the will leaves the income from his investments, which currently comes to about four hundred-fifty thousand a year, to his wife, Rachel. She also gets his life insurance money – a million – and of course the property. There are two small bequests to charities too."

"And the son? Jason?"

"He gets the business and business assets. To be frank, they're both going to be doing very well financially."

Four

"So, the mother or the son could be involved in this," Patricia said. Luke and Grant had gotten back from the interview with Christine Kramer. The three of them were sitting in the station's small conference room, going over the sheaf of papers they'd already started to gather on the Clemons case.

"Well, they both win big financially according to the lawyer," Luke said.

'I agree," Grant added. "Most murders are like that – domestic. And lots of times it's about money."

Patricia saw Jason again in her mind. Remote, hard-faced, barely said a word. And his mother, moving more like a robot than a human. Hard to tell what either of them was thinking. "Or," she said, "they could be in it together."

"I've seen that, too," Grant said. "Let's keep that in mind. What else do we have on Clemons?" He looked expectantly at Patricia.

"A basic check shows no criminal background, at least not in Pennsylvania. Motor vehicle report's clean, too. One speeding ticket two years ago, but nothing since then. I haven't heard back yet on former marriages or name changes."

"Phone records?"

"I got the green light on that and sent it through. We should be getting those records in a day or two."

"OK, anything else?"

"Just the basics we already knew. Address, place of business, it all checks out."

"All right. We'll start digging deeper. We'll start tomorrow with his widow. And don't worry, Stanley, you'll get to play, too."
Patricia ducked her head a little. Was it that obvious?

Two hours later she was finally ready to clock out and go home. Her shoulders and neck ached from an afternoon of desk work. Maybe she'd ask Becky if she wanted to go to the gym. They'd only been there once in the last ten days – pitiful.

When she got home, though, Becky was curled up, sound asleep on the sofa. She looked absolutely exhausted and Patricia didn't have the heart to wake her partner up. She went as silently as she could into the kitchen and took a bottle of water from the refrigerator. She was holding it, staring out the window, when a sleepy voice behind her said, "When'd you get home?"
"I'm sorry. Did I wake you up?"
"No, I wouldn't even have known you were home, but I saw your purse on the chair."
"Yeah, I just got back about ten minutes ago or so."
"So how was your day?"
"It was a desk day. I hate them. I'm all knotted up. In fact, I was going to ask if you want to hit the gym."
"OK. Just let me wake up first."

The workout had been exactly the right idea, Patricia thought later. There was something about the effort of lifting weights, using the leg machines and working the rowing machine that swept out all of the cobwebs. It made you feel clean, even if you were sweaty. When she and Becky were finished with the machines, they showered and changed into jeans and t-shirts.

"You hungry?" Becky asked.

"Dying. Let's get some burgers. My treat."

"And waste all that exercise? What are you, on the TV Cop Diet now?"

"Yes, and this time, order your own fries. I don't want you stealing mine."

"Who, me?"

Patricia stirred one of her fries through the small blob of ketchup on her plate. "Do you think I'm being paranoid?"

"The truth?"

"Of course the truth."

"OK, then yes. I think you are being a little paranoid. So you didn't go the lawyer's office today. It doesn't sound like it was personal. Besides, background checks are important. So are phone records and all of that."

"I know. I just don't want to be Daisy the Desk Damsel, batting my eyelashes. Ugh!"

"I don't know. You have cute eyes."

"Shut up!" Patricia balled up a napkin and threw it across the table. Becky caught it neatly and tossed it back.

"But seriously," she said after taking a sip of her water. 'You really think that woman might have done it?"

"Family members do kill each other, Becky."

"I know," Becky said, looking down at her plate for a minute. "But aren't there other people who could have done it too?"

"Yeah, of course. But there's something about that family."

"You're so suspicious."

"Probably, but it's like you've told me about lab findings. If you hear the sound of hoofs, think "horse" first."

When they got back to their apartment, Patricia flopped down on the sofa and turned on the TV. After a few minutes of surfing, she found a movie she'd seen twice already – just the perfect thing to help her unwind. Becky sat down beside her on the sofa.
"Didn't we see this one?"
"Yeah, I just didn't feel like thinking."
Becky leaned her head on Patricia's shoulder and tucked her feet up on the sofa. "Me either," she said. Then she put her arm around Patricia and kissed the back of her neck. "Who needs thinking anyway?"
"Highly overrated," Patricia murmured. This complete letting go of herself was still a little new to her, but right now, it was exactly what she needed. The TV voices faded into the background as she turned towards Becky. Those green eyes were almost hypnotic as she leaned in for a kiss.

Their lovemaking was slow and warm, like a hearth on a cold night. Patricia hadn't felt safe since Serena's death, but Becky was a haven. The sex was exciting, but more than that, Becky anchored her. When they were finished, she lay awake for a long time with Becky's head resting just under her chin. She could feel her quiet, even breathing matching her own and slowly, she drifted to sleep, her fingers twined through Becky's hair.

The doorbell startled Rachel and she nearly dropped the pile of clothes she'd been folding. A lot of

[71]

people hated to do laundry, but Rachel found it soothing. "You should pack Ron's things away," Lina had said. "They're just terrible reminders." But it wasn't time. Not yet. That would come another day. There was the doorbell again. Rachel climbed the stairs from the laundry room and went to the front door. Two people. One was that cop who'd come to see her before. The other one was a man Rachel didn't recognize. Probably another cop though. She wiped her hands on her jeans and opened the door.

"Good morning, Mrs. Clemons," the woman said. "You and I have met, and this is Detective Grant. May we come in?" What were they doing here? "Yes, of course." Say something else. Say anything else. "I'm – I'm afraid I'm in the middle of laundry. The place is a mess."

"Not a problem." This from the man Grant. Show them in. Sit them down.

Once the three were seated in the living room (Tea? Coffee? Are you sure?), Rachel said, "Why – how can I help you?"

"It's about your husband, Mrs. Clemons."

"You've already asked me questions about him."

"I know, Ma'am, but we're taking another look at his death. We believe he's been murdered."

"Are you sure?" How stupid was that? Of course they were sure or they wouldn't be here.

"Yes, Ma'am, we are. And we'd like your help." Why wasn't the man saying anything? He was just sitting there. Why was he staring at her?

"I – of course I want to help." That sounded better.

"Thank you. I know this is a hard time for you." Was that a flash of sympathy in the woman's eyes?

"But we do have some questions."

"All right."

"Do you know anyone who would have wanted to hurt your husband – or you?"

"Me? No. I mean, I can't imagine anyone wanting to hurt me."

"And your husband?"

"No. Ron was – he made friends easily. Everybody liked him. He was more social than I am, to tell the truth."

"No threats, odd phone calls, anything like that? Please think carefully."

"No, not at all."

"No visitors you didn't know?"

"I keep telling you! Nothing!"

"Had he taken any trips lately?"

"Business trips? Actually, yes. He went to New York a couple of weeks ago. A client, I think. He said the company might be doing publicity for them. They even sent some people down here on the day he…he died."

"And that was when?"

"He left on the 18th of last month. He was back two days later."

"And was that normal for him – to travel?"

"Oh, yes. But just for the real top-money clients. The ones who didn't want to deal with a rep. Sometimes he went if there was a problem, too, to smooth things over. His company had some top-money clients in New York, and some in Wilmington and Baltimore, too."

"Do you know who he met with in New York?"

"Sorry. You'll have to talk to Emma Yeats – that's his assistant – about that. She has all of that information."

"We will."

[73]

Now Officer Stanley started to look a little uncomfortable. Her tone changed too. Something was coming. "Mrs. Clemons, I have to ask you a few other questions."

"All right." The knots in her stomach again. That look on the cop's face. Just like at the memorial service. This cop wanted to get her.

"What was your marriage like?" Our marriage. Ron coming home after work. Ron's car starting in the morning. The shuffle of the newspaper. The TV on. When will you be back? I should be back Thursday. Love you.

"It was stable. Ron was a steady guy."

"No problems?"'

"Problems? You mean fights? Of course, we had disagreements. You're not married, are you? If you were, you'd know that every couple gets into it sometimes."

"Anything serious?"

"Why are you asking me all these questions about our marriage? We weren't unhappy if that's what you're getting at. Wait a minute. Do you think I killed Ron?"

"Did you?"

"What the – No! How dare you! You can't come in here and accuse me like that. I'd like you both to leave. Now."

That did it. They slowly got up, thanked her for her time and left. Good. That was easier than it might have been. They'd cast a shadow over everything. Well, at least they were gone.

Grant drove silently, while Patricia looked miserably out the passenger side window. Neither said a word for the first few minutes. Finally, she said, "I blew it, didn't I?"

"It could have gone better," Grant said curtly.

The one thing Grant wouldn't want was a bunch of excuses. There were none anyway.

"You don't get anything from people when it sounds like you're accusing them. And now she may not talk to us again without a lawyer."

"I guess I thought –"

"Doesn't matter what you thought. We have no solid evidence against her. We don't even know where she was when her husband was killed. You jumped the gun on this one."

"I'm sorry. I know. I screwed it up."

Grant gave her a sideways glance. His face softened almost imperceptibly. "It's not the end of the world, Stanley. We'll still get what we need. And who knows? Maybe she did kill him. But from now on, you wait until you have evidence before you accuse."

Patricia nodded, not trusting herself to say anything.

They pulled into the police station's parking lot. Patricia slunk into the back entrance, hoping nobody would talk to her. She was lucky until she got to her desk. When she sat down and turned her computer on, Luke said, "So how'd it go?"

"Don't ask, OK?"

"That good, huh?"

"Honestly, I don't want to talk about it right now."

"It can't be that bad. How about a beer after work? I'll even buy."

"Yeah, maybe."

An hour later Grant walked over to their desks. "You two eat lunch yet?"

"Just about to." Luke said.

"Good. Grab something and then we'll tackle Mid-Atlantic. We need to talk to the people our guy worked with."

Patricia looked steadily at her computer, hoping it would hide her face. She was still smarting from this morning.

"I want you both ready in half an hour," Grant said.

This time Patricia couldn't resist. "Both?"

"Yeah, both. Enders will do the interviews. You'll go over the client lists. Find out who Clemons saw recently. I want names, addresses, the whole thing."

Right. Busywork. Well, she deserved that. And besides, at least she wasn't exiled to her desk for the rest of the day. It wasn't good, but at least she'd be doing something.

Trent Rakins sat at his sleek mahogany desk. Across from him was Wade Messner. "If we go in that direction, Trent, we're going to have to change a lot more than just our client list." Wade shifted in his seat, looked down at the papers he had in front of him, and said, "It's also going to affect our reputation."

"I know there are going to have to be some big changes. But I really think we need to re-consider our market. We've been missing out on a lot of accounts because of Ron's short-sightedness."

"I wouldn't exactly call it short-sighted, Trent. Ron wanted to position us as a boutique company. If we go for a different market, we could lose our more exclusive clients."

Trent leaned back slightly in his black leather desk chair, templed his fingers and smiled.

"Look, Wade, you're Head of Vendor Accounts. That's your area of expertise. We need you to focus on that. Let me and the sales team handle our clients. You don't need to worry about that end of the business."

Wade half rose from his chair. "Don't 'manage' me, Trent. I'm being serious here. We have a top-of-the-line image. I don't think we should risk that just to pick up some new clients."

"It's not that simple, Wade, and you'd know that if you were on the sales side of things. There's a limited pool of penthouse-suite clients. We need to expand our base, so it makes sense to look for another kind of market."

"But what happens when our current clients see that change? They like being branded as VIP and they like feeling that they're doing business with a select agency. They may very well switch to a competitor."

"I hear what you're saying, Wade. But what you don't understand is there's a much larger base of slightly lower-end clients. If we go for that market, we'll be fishing in a lot bigger pond. Can you understand that?"

"I'm not stupid, Trent!"

"Well, then –"

Just then there was a knock on Trent's closed office door, and it opened slightly. His assistant Max Anselm stuck his head around the door. "Sorry to bother you, Trent. There are some people here to see you."

"I'm in a meeting, Max. Can't you see that?"

"They're police."

Trent took a breath. "Sorry," he muttered. "OK, I'll be with them in a minute. I think we're done here, Wade."

"No, we're not." Wade said, setting his jaw firmly.

"I don't have any more time for this. It'll have to be another day." Trent got up and strode towards the door without bothering to look behind him.

By the time he got to the reception area, Trent had focused himself. He greeted Grant and Luke briskly. "Sorry you had to wait. Busy morning. Let's sit in my office." They followed him back to his office, where he drew up a second chair in front of his desk.

"Now, what can I do for you?"

"We're looking into the death of Ronald Clemons," Luke said.

"I thought you might be. It's been a major blow to all of us. We're trying to pick up the pieces around here, but it'll be hard. He was one of a kind. How's his wife doing?"

"She's managing. We have a couple of questions for you."

"Shoot."

"When did you last see Mr. Clemons?"

"Let me see…I think it was the day before he died. We had a meeting late that afternoon."

"And you didn't see him the morning he died?"

"No, I went into the city that morning to see a client. Max – my assistant – called and told me what happened."

"How did he seem when you last saw him?"

"Ron? Fine. I mean, normal. Busy, like always, but nothing seemed wrong."

"Do you know if he was in the office on the morning he died?"

Trent smiled. "Sorry, but I don't keep tabs on everybody. I'll bet his assistant would know, though. Emma Yeats. She's got his schedule."

"We'll talk to her."

"Look," Trent glanced at his watch. "I'm sorry, but I have a meeting in a few minutes. I'm not sure how helpful I can be anyway. I wasn't here the day Ron died."

"We appreciate your time, Mr. Rakins," Luke and Grant rose, shook hands and left the office. Trent watched them go, then shook his head slightly, focused again, and opened up the presentation files he'd need for his next meeting.

"You see that guy?" Grant murmured to Luke as they left the office. He gestured with his head toward Wade, who was just leaving the men's room.

"Yeah," Luke said.

"We need to talk to him next. He was leaving Trent Rakins' office when we got there, and he looked pissed off. I want to know about him."

"Got it." They turned and followed Wade as he went down first one corridor and then the next towards his office.

"Excuse me," Luke said when they got close enough. He showed Wade his police identification, and then asked, "Could we speak to you for a minute?"

"Um, of course," Wade said as he unlocked his office door. "Come in."

He gestured towards two chairs and Grant and Luke sat down and glanced around. It wasn't as richly-appointed an office as Rakins' was, but it was neat and orderly, with pine shelves behind a matching pine desk.

"How can I help you?"

"It's about Ronald Clemons' death," said Luke.

"Oh, yes, of course. An awful thing. I liked him very much. But I thought he had a heart attack. Is – is there something wrong?"

"We're looking into his death a little more closely, and we'd appreciate your answering a few questions."

"Of course. I'll help in any way I can. Ron was a friend, and his death's been very upsetting."

"I'm sure it has been." Luke glanced down at his notes. "And your name is?"

"Wade Messner. I'm Head of Vendor Services here. And yes, Ron's death has been terrible. But honestly, I can't say it's a complete shock to find that he's been murdered."

Luke looked up quickly. He noticed that Grant was paying close attention, too. "Can you tell me what you mean by that?"

Wade leaned slightly forward. "Well," he began confidentially, "I was a friend of Ron's. I know how hard he worked to get the company where it is. He wanted us to have an elite image and that's what we've got. Thanks to him we have a truly fine client list. But not everyone shared his vision."

"Oh, no?"

"No. Some people here wanted the company to go after a different market; to be honest, a less exclusive one. And that would upset a lot of our clients. Ron knew that. He knew how important the VIP thing is to the people we work with. Let's just say some people thought he was standing in the way. I didn't. I liked where we'd positioned

ourselves. I've tried to tell him, too. He just doesn't
want to hear."

"Who is 'he?'"

Wade lowered his head for a moment and then said,
"Trent Rakins. He wants to move the company in
exactly the opposite direction from Ron. He and
Ron went around about it more than once. If
anyone's happy Ron's out of the way, it's Trent."

"That's very helpful. Thank you."

"So, are you going to arrest him? I mean, he really
had a good motive. He hated Ron."

"It certainly sounds as though he had a good
motive."

"You see? I think so too. You *are* going to arrest
him, aren't you?"

"It's a possibility."

Grant glared swiftly at Luke and then said, "Well,
we won't take up any more of your time. We
appreciate your help."

"Of course. I'm happy to be of whatever help I
can."

After they'd left the office, Luke said, "What was
that about?"

Grant drew him aside, pointed to the empty
conference room they'd just passed and said in a
quiet but angry voice, 'In there.'

They went into the conference room and Grant shut
the door. Then he turned to Luke and said, "You do
not talk to anyone about whether or not we are
going to arrest someone. Right now, we're getting
evidence. That's all. And even if we had more
evidence, even if all of it were against Rakins, you
do *not* discuss it with anyone. Do you know how

[81]

quickly the word is going to spread? If Rakins turns out to have nothing to do with this, we could be in for serious trouble."

"But after what this guy just said to us, I thought…"

"You thought wrong. Do the math. The guy's furious when he leaves Rakins' office. Not twenty minutes later he's all excited to tell us why he thinks Rakins might have wanted to kill our victim."

"So he's got a grudge."

"Exactly. You can't take what people say at face value, Enders. Always look at what's in it for them when they tell you anything. And no matter what, you say nothing to anyone you interview about the investigation. Is that clear?"

"Clear."

Grant opened the conference room door and said, "Let's go see how Stanley's doing with that client list." Luke followed his boss without saying a word.

Patricia had spent the last half hour going through Clemons' list of past and current clients. Emma Yeats had provided her with copies of contracts, emails and other communication, and she had sorted them into categories based on amount of contact. Later she would read them more carefully and see if any of them might have a grudge or another reason to want Clemons dead. It had been a little tedious, but as Grant had said, it all mattered.

She looked up when Grant and Luke entered the room. One glance at Luke's face and she knew something had gone wrong. No, don't open your mouth, she told herself. You'll find out soon enough. The two men sat down, and Grant said, "How'd it go?"

"There's plenty of information here about dates and times of meetings and so on. Client contact information too. Nothing's really jumping out at me though."

"Who was the last client he met with?"

"His last scheduled meeting was with a rep from Spenglar Galleries, out of New York. Apparently, they sent someone down to finalize some of the paperwork to have Mid-Atlantic do their publicity. That was the meeting he was going to when he died."

"And before that?"

"The day before he died, his last meeting was with a company called WorldWide Living. They're a high-end real-estate outfit. Second homes, vacation homes, that kind of thing. Seems straightforward though. It looks like that was just a yearly check-in meeting. It seems Clemons did that with some of their top clients."

"All right. Anything else?"

"Nothing that screams out."

"Get copies of all of those files, just in case."

"Got it." Grant didn't look as though he wanted any input, so Patricia picked up the files she'd spread out on the table and went in search of a copy machine.

Ten minutes and one helpful receptionist later, Patricia returned to the conference room with copies of the client information. While she put the original files back into their folders, Grant laid out their next steps. Luke gazed steadily at the table.

"We've got two angles on this case. Who wanted our guy dead, and who had access to digitoxin. We have to wait for the final toxicology report to find out exactly how he got the poison. And that could take time. But let's at least start narrowing things down."

"What about finding out what he did that morning? I mean more closely than we have," Patricia said, trying to redeem herself at least a little.

Grant nodded. "We do need to do that. We'll have to find out exactly what he ate or drank, where he got it, and who gave it to him. We'll start digging deeper tomorrow. For today, let's at least get a rough idea of where he was that morning. Enders, I want you to put together a list of what we already know about that. Stanley, you'll do a check on where those clients are located. Find out if any of them are located close enough to be in the area that morning."

Luke and Patricia made notes. When Grant had finished, they gathered their files and notebooks to leave.

The trip back to the station was uncomfortably silent. Whatever had gone wrong between Luke and the boss had soured everything, Patricia thought. Not that she had made things much cheerier. Once she and Luke had settled themselves at their desks, she glanced over at him from time to time, but he radiated 'Leave me alone!' so she decided to give him space. She didn't have a whole lot of time to wonder anyway. She really wanted to get back in Grant's good graces, and that would mean getting the information he asked her to get.

She printed off a map of the area, and then put dots in places where all of the most local clients were located. There were only two with offices close to

Paoli, but three others were within easy striking distance if the client had wanted to make an effort. And any of the clients' reps could have stayed overnight locally if they wanted to. It didn't help that the list she had was only the list of clients that Clemons himself had served. There were many others. That didn't narrow things down much, but at least she could find out if any of Clemons' own clients had sent their reps officially. The next hour and went by quickly as she called her way down the list. The effort didn't get her very far though. Only one client, Spenglar Galleries, had a rep in the area on the day of the murder, and Clemons was on his way to that meeting when he died. It was possible that the rep could have met with Clemons earlier and killed him, but that didn't make sense given where he was found. She made a note to herself, though, to find out from Luke exactly when Clemons had gotten to his office that morning and when he'd left.

Luke. What had happened with him and Grant? He'd barely spoken a word since they got back to the station, and she hadn't wanted to ask. She decided to start simple.

"You get anywhere on Clemons' schedule the day he was killed?"

"Some. I have a rough outline."

"Good. I know he was supposed to meet with a rep from that gallery in New York. I'm just wondering if he could have had time to meet early in the day, before the scheduled meeting."

"Don't see how, if the wife's telling the truth. She says he left the house at seven-thirty. Then the assistant says he met with her at eight-fifteen.

[85]

That's not a lot of time, especially if he was at the building before he met with his assistant."
"No, it's not. Just wanting to cover all the bases."
"Yeah, I know."
"You ready for that beer now?"
"Let me just finish up here. Ten more minutes?"
"Sounds good."

Half an hour later, Luke and Patricia were sitting at a small table at Paco's Cantina. There was a pitcher of beer, a large bowl of warm tortilla chips, and three small bowls of salsas between them. The tables and chairs were of pine, and the pine walls were decorated with Diego Rivera and Frida Kahlo prints. Patricia had been here before, but this was Luke's first time.

Patricia dipped a chip in the *salsa verde* and said, "OK, spill. What's wrong?"
"Give me a break. I haven't even had a sip of my beer yet."
"Let's fix that." Patricia poured both of them a beer and they touched glasses. For a few minutes, they sipped their beers and kept the conversation to the Phillies' chances that season. Luke stretched his legs out and finally seemed to relax a little.
When their glasses were about half empty, Patricia said, "All right, you've had twenty minutes to have some tortilla chips and some beer. Now tell me what happened today with Grant."
"I fucked up, OK? I messed up an interview pretty badly and Grant reamed me for it."
Patricia waited. Luke looked away and then back at her.
"Sorry," he said, in a quieter voice this time. "I totally blew it and I'm not exactly proud of myself."

"Couldn't have been worse than what I did. So, you tell me and then I'll tell you. Promise. OK?"

"Deal." Luke told her what had happened with Wade Messner. When he was finished, she grimaced sympathetically. She knew what it felt like.

"So, I told my tale," Luke said. "Your turn. C'mon, please don't let me think I'm the only one who screwed up today."

"Not by a long shot." Patricia told him about the visit to Rachel Clemons' house. "Grant was right,' she finished. 'I should never have accused her like that. What was I thinking?"

"I know what you mean. Some days are best forgotten."

"Amen to that."

Five

Patricia was glad that she had to be at work early the next morning, in spite of what had happened the day before. She didn't want Grant to think she was a crybaby and she didn't want him to think she was defensive. It wasn't easy though. Word had gotten around, as it always did, that something had happened, and she had to deal with a few strange looks as she came into the station. She ignored the looks as best she could, sat down at her desk and turned on her computer.

Twenty minutes later, the station's receptionist-on-duty stopped by her desk. "These came for you last night."
"Oh, thanks," Patricia said, and took the set of papers. The wireless service provider had sent over Ronald Clemons' records. She looked through them for a few minutes and then put them down. Then she went over each one again, this time much more carefully. She took a pen from her desk tray and started circling numbers.

"What's that?" Luke asked. He drew a bagel out of a paper bag and put it on her desk.
"Thanks," she smiled. "How'd you know I didn't eat breakfast?"
"Just figured. Anyway, what do you have there?"
"Ronald Clemons' telephone records."
"Yeah? Anything good?"
"Actually, there might be. You think Grant's willing to talk to us this morning?"

"He'll be unhappier if we don't tell him whatever you found."

Patricia guessed that Luke was right. She nodded, picked up the papers and said, "Let's go into the lion's den."

Grant looked up when they got to his desk. "You got something I should see?" he asked.

"These are Clemons' telephone records. We thought you'd want to know about them."

"OK, let's hear it.'"

"Two of the numbers I already recognized: his home number and his office number. Most of the others only pop up here and there. We can track them down if you want, but I didn't see a pattern. But here's one that keeps popping up. He called it five times in the week before he died – each time for more than fifteen minutes. And he got seven calls from the same number. Two of them were really short – maybe the caller left messages. But the others were longer. Total of ten actual conversations."

Grant reached out his hand for the papers, which Patricia gave him. He looked them over, looked at Patricia and said, "Interesting. And it's not a local area code. I want us to talk to whoever it is. Could be a client. Could be anyone. Follow up, Stanley, and let me know. If we need to, we'll do an interview. Enders, I want you to start following the money. I got a court order this morning to look at Clemons' personal finances and the company finances. We'll start personal. I want you to find out who he owed and how much. Also look for any strange deposit or withdrawal patterns. Now get out of here, both of you."

They got out of there.

The voice on the other end was young, firm and masculine. "Yes, this is Victor Wagner. Who is this please?"
Patricia identified herself.
"The police? I'm sorry – I don't understand.'"
"'Do you know Ronald Clemons?" A long silence. She must have hit paydirt, although it was sometimes hard to tell over the phone.
"I –what is this about?"
"Sir, if you could just tell me whether you're acquainted with Ronald Clemons?"
"Yes. I guess you could say I am."
"We'd like to speak to you in person, sir."
"All right. Where are you located?"

When Victor Wagner arrived, Patricia seated him in one of the interview rooms. She badly wanted to do this interview, but it would be Grant's call. "You found him, you talk to him." he said. "I'll sit in, though."
"Got it." That was good news. She hadn't known how long it would be before she'd be talking to witnesses again. She felt lucky to have a boss who would let her try again.

The interview room was utilitarian, with light-green painted walls, a rectangular table and straight-backed chairs. It wasn't made for comfort, but it was clean and there was enough light that it didn't feel too much like a cell. Patricia took a long look at Wagner before she began. She realized then that she'd seen him at the memorial service. He was of medium height, with wavy light-brown hair, pale gray eyes and a small, neatly-clipped moustache. He didn't look rich enough to be one of Clemons' clients. It would be interesting to find out how he fit into all this. After they'd greeted each other, Wagner asked,

"Do I need a lawyer? Is there a problem?"

"You're free to call a lawyer if you wish, Mr. Wagner. But you aren't under arrest. I asked you to come in because we're investigating the death of Ronald Clemons, and you had several telephone conversations with him in the days before he died. I'm hoping you'll tell us what they were about." An almost imperceptible nod from Grant. Good. She'd started off on the right note.

"To be honest, those telephone calls were private. I'd rather not discuss them. I don't think they have any bearing on your investigation anyway."

"Maybe not, but it would still be helpful if you'd let us know what you talked about."

Wagner shifted in his seat and looked around. Then he looked back at Patricia and sighed. "All right. I'll tell you. But please – this has to be confidential."

"It will be."

He nodded and then began. "Ronald Clemons is – was – my father. I didn't know that until six months ago. He and my mother got together soon after she got out of college. It didn't last. They ended things before she knew she was pregnant with me. By the time she found out, he'd gone to Europe for a trip, and she lost track of him. It wasn't as easy then as it is now to keep in touch. Anyway, when I was three, she married my stepfather. I had a good life. I never really thought about who my 'real' father was. I always thought of Dave – my stepfather – as my dad. And Mom didn't make a big deal about it either. I guess she didn't want to confuse me. Don't get me wrong. She didn't lie to me. I always knew that Dave wasn't my biological father. And she said when I was ready to ask questions, I could. But like I said, I had no burning desire to find out about my biological father. Life went on, you know? I moved to Chicago, started working at the Stock Exchange there."

He paused for a minute and took a sip of the coffee they'd brought him. When he didn't continue, Patricia encouraged him. "But something changed?"
He nodded. "You could say that. I fell in love. Syd's great, too. She's beautiful, smart, the whole thing. We got married two years ago. And now she's pregnant. We both want to know whether the baby's at risk for anything. That means hereditary health background, and that's what got me interested in finding Ronald Clemons."
"Did your mother tell you his name?"
"Yes, not long before she died – cancer. She didn't have any animosity. She'd never told him about me, and she always said that was her choice. And with Dave around, it didn't really matter, at least not to me. But with a baby on the way, well, I wanted to know."
"So how did you track him down?"
"I did a lot myself, and I hired a private investigator for the rest. It's not that hard these days."
"And you talked to him?"
"Yes, a few times. At first, he didn't believe me when I told him who I was. But I promised him I didn't want anything from him, and I persuaded him to meet me. I even said we could do a paternity test. He agreed to that, and when the results came

[92]

in, well, that was that. When we met in person, he said I looked just like Mom. We had some good talks. He was going to send me medical records, the whole thing, I think."

"He told you about his family?"

'That's just it. He did. And that's why I want this to stay private. I don't think he told his wife about me and that's fine. It all happened before he met her, anyway, and like I said, he didn't even know about me until I contacted him. I don't want to disrupt his family, especially not now that he's dead."

Patricia managed a surreptitious glance at Grant. He moved a hand slightly towards the door. That was his 'finish up' signal and she agreed with it. They didn't have any solid basis for suspecting this guy and he'd come of his own volition. Best end the conversation on good terms if they could. She gave Grant the slightest of nods and said,

"All right, Mr. Wagner. I appreciate your coming in. I don't think we have any other questions for right now. How long are you staying in the area?"

"Until you called, I was planning to go back to Palatine – that's a suburb of Chicago – where Syd and I live, tomorrow."

Patricia wasn't sure exactly what to say to that, but Grant stepped in smoothly. "I don't see any reason for you to change your plans. Just make sure we have your address. And please don't travel anywhere else without letting us know, at least for now."

"I won't. And you will keep this confidential? Like I said, I don't want to hurt anybody."

"We will."

When Wagner had gone, Patricia went back to her desk to fill Luke in on the interview. Grant said he'd join them in a few minutes.

"Unbelievable," Luke said when she'd finished.

"Yeah, not exactly what I'd have expected either." Luke slid down a little in his chair, stuck his feet out and dropped his arms onto the chair's arms. "So this guy," he said, thinking aloud, "knows his biological father is out there somewhere. He finds out where he is, makes contact, asks for medical records. Maybe finds out Clemons has money, wants to go for the gold?"

"I doubt it," Patricia said. "Remember, you told me Clemons didn't change his will. Why would this guy kill him before he changed the will if that was what he thought would happen?"

"Good point. OK. But still, we ought to check the money angle."

"I think so too," Grant said as he joined them. "Money makes even the nicest people do some pretty nasty things. Enders, what have you found out about Clemons' finances?"

"Nothing really unusual. The day-to-day stuff looks normal. Small ATM withdrawals, credit cards paid up, your basic trip to Hawaii for vacation. Oh, and one trip to Paris. Also presumably for vacation. Nothing a guy like him couldn't afford. He has a gilt-edged retirement account, but there haven't been any withdrawals from it and only the regular deposits."

"What about the company's finances?"

"Still waiting for those. They should be in later today or tomorrow."

"OK, so for now, it doesn't look on the surface like this Victor Wagner was getting any money. I still want his background though," Grant said. "His wife's too. And it's not just the money. Biological father goes off, not in the picture, gets rich. That could make anyone resentful. I want to know more about these people."

Patricia did too. Wagner had seemed like a nice enough person with a logical reason to want to find his biological father. But who knew what might be going on under the surface? She made a note to herself to add any psychiatric reports or closed juvey records to her list of things to look for in Wagner's past. Social worker reports too, if there were any. You never knew what might turn up.

Then Patricia had another thought. Something had been nagging at her and now she was annoyed at not having thought of it before. She scribbled another note to herself and started to make some phone calls to get the authorizations she'd need for the background checks Grant wanted. Getting through to the right people and downloading the right forms took about forty minutes, but she finally got the paperwork sent through. Once she got the approvals, she'd let Grant know and she and Luke could get started.

Now she decided to pursue her other idea. Luke had left to observe an interview on a shoplifting case, so this would be a good time. She did an Internet search for some information and downloaded what she found. By the time Luke got back twenty minutes later, she had papers spread all over her desk. He took at her desk, then at her computer screen. "Are you opening a garden shop?" he asked.
"Foxglove."
"What?"

"Foxglove. The initial tox report said Ronald Clemons died of digitoxin poisoning, right? Well, I found out that often comes from the foxglove family of plants. And foxglove grows fairly easily around here, so it wouldn't be hard to get your hands on it."

"Fair enough. But you can get digitoxin in other ways, can't you?"

"You can, but it wouldn't be easy. Doctors don't prescribe it in this country. You'd have to know who to talk to if you wanted to get your hands on some. If you're a killer, wouldn't you rather do something that's easier and calls less attention to yourself?"

"But wouldn't you have to have some knowledge of herbs and how to use them?"

"Not necessarily. From what I read," Patricia waved a hand at the papers on her desk, "it's not that hard to get poison from these plants. That's what makes them so highly toxic. I haven't read everything I've got yet, but I think anyone could use them easily."

"That doesn't narrow things down a lot."

"Well, we could at least find out if anyone involved has foxglove growing in the yard or nearby."

"True."

"I have to clock out now, but I'll get on it tomorrow."

"Sounds good. I'll get busy on those company financials if they're in tomorrow."

Patricia didn't usually leave early, but today she had an appointment with Dr. Zara. She'd been doing well for a while now, but Ronald Clemons' murder had touched something off. She'd even snapped at Becky that morning, which she rarely did. They'd talked it over, but it wasn't something she was proud of doing. And she didn't want it to happen again.

Now she pulled into the parking lot of the small building where Dr. Zara had her office. She felt a little better just being there, but she knew this wasn't going to be an easy session. They never were. She locked her car and went inside to the office, which was on the second floor. Ten minutes later Dr. Zara opened the door to her office and saw Patricia. "Come on in," she said

Patricia nodded and followed her therapist into her private room. The pale green couch, light walls and muted pastel prints on the walls were all designed to have a calming effect and they usually did. Dr. Zara closed the door, smiled, and said, "It's good to see you, Patricia. Have a seat and we'll catch up." She flipped her gray ponytail behind her back and settled into her chair.

Patricia made herself comfortable on the couch and then said, "I'm wondering if I'm slipping back."
"What do you mean by 'slipping back?'"
"Not moving on with my life. Getting stuck again. I keep thinking about Serena. Little things, you know, like how we used to help each other study. Or the doughnuts she liked. That kind of thing. I'm – it's all coming back right now, and it's making it hard to move ahead."
"Grief is like that sometimes, Patricia. You do better. You feel better. And then you don't for a while. And then you start to feel a little better again. And the next time, maybe you don't slip back as far. It's not a straight line."

"I know. Well, I know that's what you've said before. But it's just been hitting me again this past week."

"Do you think there's a reason for that? A birthday? Maybe your anniversary with Serena?"

"No, not any of that. I used to mark that stuff on my calendar, but not now. No, I think it's because of a case I'm working."

Dr. Zara waited silently. Police cases were tricky things, and even though her sessions were private, there was always the question of how much a cop would be willing to say. After a few minutes, Patricia found a way to tell her. "OK, I'm on this murder case. A guy's been killed. He's got a widow and a grown son. It's – it's a good thing for a cop as young as I am to be even on a murder case, so that part is good. Doing things like background checks, information searches, talking to some of the people in the guy's life, no problem. I can do my job. And I *like* it. I like trying to find out what happened. But then I had to talk to the widow and the son, and I fell apart. I barely held it together, asked some stupid questions, and nearly got in big trouble at work. I just didn't focus."

"It sounds like those interviews really got to you."

"They did. And I mean, they were just interviews. I've done interviews before. And I've been doing others that haven't bothered me at all."

"So, what made these different?"

Patricia thought for a long minute. Rachel Clemons' wooden expression. Jason Clemons' hard, unyielding features. Their faces at the memorial service. Those empty eyes. "It was me. I saw me right after Serena was killed. It brought it all back. Those people are hurting just like I did."

"That makes sense."

"And you want to know the worst thing? I can't do a damned thing about it." Now the tears that had been pricking the back of Patricia's eyes made it all the way to the front. She pulled a tissue from the box on the wood-and-glass table in front of the couch and dabbed her eyes. "I can't make those people feel any better. And the whole thing just makes me think of what happened to Serena all over. I almost puked the other day after one of those interviews." She dabbed her eyes again and said, "It makes me scared."

"Scared of what?"

"Scared that I can't do my job. Scared that I'll lose it every time I'm on a case. If I can't handle my emotions when I'm on the job, I won't be any good. I'll end up on Traffic Patrol or something."

"How many murders have you investigated as a cop?"

"This is my first."

"Right. So you weren't as prepared this first time as you will be. You're learning. And it's OK to be learning. Nobody expects you to be perfect right away. Or ever, for that matter."

"But what if it happens again? What if I lose it next time I talk to that woman? Or another widow?"

"You'll take what you're learning now, and you'll use it to respond better next time. Just like you learn any skill. Let's talk about what you can do when you start feeling that way, so you'll be able to handle it next time without feeling scared."

After her session, Patricia went home. Fortunately, Becky hadn't gotten there yet. She loved Becky, and she saw a real possibility for a future with her. But Becky wasn't always comfortable with Patricia's therapy sessions. "You can tell me anything," Becky would say. And she was right about that. She understood, too, that sometimes people needed professional help. It was a little harder for her, though, to really accept that there were things her partner would rather say to a therapist than to her. Becky loved her, though, and had never gotten in the way of her therapy. It was just a little awkward at times. Hopefully she'd start to feel better about it. Or Patricia would get to the point where she didn't feel the need of help. Or both.

She flipped through the mail she'd collected on her way to their apartment. Nothing much this time. She tossed it on the living room coffee table and went into the kitchen. She opened the refrigerator to see what there was for dinner. Not an awful lot, but enough to put together an omelet. And that was about all she was in the mood for, anyway. She was pulling out the eggs, scallions and tomatoes when she heard the door click open.

"That you?" she called out.

"No, it's Godzilla."

Patricia laughed. "Glad you're here, Godzilla. I hope monsters eat omelets."

"This one does. And this monster even brings home a bottle of wine to go with it."

"Then you are more than welcome to come in and pillage."

Becky came into the kitchen and put the bottle of wine into the refrigerator. She gave Patricia a quick hug and said, "How was your day? Dare I ask?" "Could have been worse. And it's just gotten better."

The next morning, Rachel sat quietly in her favorite place at the kitchen counter. It wasn't quite warm enough to leave the windows open at night but in an hour or so, she'd be able to let in the morning air. She sipped her coffee and stared at the newspaper headlines in front of her. Government scandals, threats of war, economic problems, it was all there, but nothing was sinking in. The haze she'd lived in since Ron's death was wearing off, but she still wasn't ready to think about anyone else's problems.

And that went for her clients, too. Tomorrow she would try to get back to work, but she'd decided to take just one more day away from them. Right now, their problems and questions seemed like so much whining, like the droning noise of a mosquito, and just about as welcome. She would have to work on that attitude before she interacted with them again.

The day stretched ahead of her, but that was almost appealing. No demands on her time, no-one asking if she was OK, no-one offering to take her out 'for her own good.' She was glad that people cared, but she was quickly getting tired of being pitied. Ron's things. That's what she would do. They needed to be sorted, and it would give her a productive chore. Was that cold? No, not really. It was necessary. Keeping Ron's clothes and other things wouldn't do

her any good. And she'd already asked Jason if he
wanted any of his father's things.

With that sense of purpose, she went up to the
bedroom and opened Ron's closet. His suits, shirts,
sports coats, trousers, shoes, all of it was still there
as though he'd be back the next day. She could
almost smell his cologne as she started to take the
shirts from their hangers. For today, she'd fold them
and box them up. She could donate them tomorrow.
She'd just folded the first few shirts when she heard
the back door open and the sound of a familiar
voice.
"Rachel, you here?"
"Upstairs, Lina. In the bedroom."

Lina joined her a moment later. "Honey, what are
you doing?" she asked.
"I'm going through Ron's things. I want to get them
ready to donate."
"Oh, you shouldn't be doing that! I can take care of
all of that for you. Now you just sit down over there
and take a break."
"Lina, I'm fine. Really. You don't need to do any of
this."
"Of course I do! You're dealing with enough right
now. You don't need this on top of everything else.
I'll handle everything."
Rachel knew this would happen if Lina came over.
Ever since their parents had died when Lina was in
college and Rachel still in high school, it had been
like that. She felt responsible for Rachel. And that
had been fine once. But now it chafed Rachel.

"Lina, I can handle it just fine. I'm really OK. Besides, I'm sure you have plenty in your own life to keep you busy."

"I don't mind." Lina began to pull Ron's clothes from the closet as she spoke. "This is too painful a job for you to handle by yourself. What are big sisters for? You go get some boxes and bags. Go on, now."

Rachel went down to the garage for boxes, then into the pantry for bags. That ought to be enough. She stood in the pantry for a minute looking at the boxes and bags that Lina had asked her to get. That Lina had told her to get. No, it just wasn't going to work. She didn't want to hurt Lina, but this couldn't go on. Not now. With a decisive nod she picked up the boxes and bags and took them upstairs. By that time Lina had taken all of Ron's shirts out of the closet and put them on the bed. Rachel put the boxes and bags down and said, "Lina, what are you doing? I didn't want the shirts all together like that. I wanted them separated."

"Oh, it's just easier this way. Besides, it doesn't matter."

"It does to me."

"Look, if you're that upset about it –"

"I'm not upset."

"Of course you are. Do you want me to put them all away again?"

"No, don't bother at this point. I'll sort them out."

"I was only trying to help, you know." Lina's miffed voice. She did mean well, but always got so easily hurt when people had different ideas and wanted to do things different ways. She took it as a personal rejection.

"I know, Lina. And I'm grateful for your help."
Rachel tried to smooth things over. "You've been
there for me all along. But right now, well, I just
want to sort these clothes in my own way. How
about you do the dress shirts and I'll do the others?"
"I guess so." Lina started to fold the rest of the dress
shirts, but she did it so briskly that Rachel knew she
was still angry. Well, there was nothing she could
do about that. Lina would have to get over it. It felt
odd though, standing up to her in that way. When
Lina was finished with the dress shirts, she said a
little sharply, "What about the rest of the clothes?"
"I'll do them later."
"Oh, well, OK. If that's how you want it." Rachel
really didn't want to deal with Lina's overprotective
nature right now. It was starting to feel as though
the whole day was going to be tainted. Something
must have shown in her face. Lina took a long look
at her and said, "You know what? Why don't I just
let you get back to this? You're obviously not in a
mood for company this morning. I can come back
later."

At another time Rachel might have protested,
saying she didn't want Lina to leave. And there
were times when she was incredibly grateful to her
older sister. But this time she didn't react that way.
"OK, that'll be fine."
Lina opened her mouth and then closed it. For the
first time in a long time, Rachel had said something
that actually stopped Lina in her tracks. That was
when they heard the knock on the door.

The two women looked at each other and Rachel
shrugged. Lina started to move down the stairs, but
Rachel held her hand up and went down instead. I

live here. I'll answer my own door. There were two men outside, each holding up a police ID badge. "Good morning, Mrs. Clemons. You remember we've met already. I'm Sergeant Grant and this is Officer Enders."

"Yes?" she challenged them. They were here again. And after she'd told them to leave the other day. First Lina and now this. They didn't listen to her either.

"We're sorry to bother you, Ma'am, but we have a few more questions."

"What questions?" No, you're not sorry to bother me. You're glad to do it. Fill in your little notebooks. Tick off the boxes. It doesn't matter. Ron is still dead.

"May we come in?"

Rachel said nothing, but opened the door all the way and gestured for them to come in. She waved them into the living room. No manners this time. They didn't belong here. "What do you want?"

"We're trying to trace Mr. Clemons' last movements. We're hoping that'll lead us to the person who killed him." That was the young one.

"I already told you he left here at seven-thirty that morning. That's all I know."

"Did he have breakfast before he left?"

"I suppose so. I can't clearly remember, but he usually did. Coffee and a muffin or something. I guess he did the same thing that day."

"Did he say anything about meeting anyone?"

"Just his assistant. He was supposed to meet with her just after eight. And then that client later on – the gallery."

"Do you know if he stopped to meet anyone on the way to his office?"

That was when Lina stepped in. "Excuse me, but how is she supposed to know that? Do you think he reported to her every five minutes?"

"It's a fair question, Lina. I'll answer it." Please, Lina, let me handle it! I know what I'm going to say. I'm not helpless. "No," Rachel said, turning back to the police officers. "He didn't say anything to me about meeting anyone on the way to the office. He mentioned that he didn't want to be late for his meeting with the gallery people, so he hoped his morning meeting at the office would go well."

"And he didn't call or text you after he left home?"

"No."

"Now if you don't mind," Lina spoke up again, "My sister is in mourning. She's just lost her husband. You people ought to be out finding his killer instead of badgering her."

The older cop gave Lina a look that somehow made her stop talking and look away. Rachel decided she ought to learn how to do that. Then he turned back to Rachel. "Ma'am, did you know the terms of your husband's will?"

"Terms? Yes, I did. He showed me a copy of his will years ago. I don't think he's changed it since Jason was in middle school." Of course they had to ask about the money. She'd always known she'd be well provided for if Ron died. Jason too. That's what he'd promised her. And then when her graphics company started to do well, he said she could live almost as well as she deserved. That was Ron.

"So, you're aware that you and your son both inherit."

"Of course. He – Ron – wanted me to know not to worry. At the time, I was just putting together the

[106]

business plan for my company. I was worried it wouldn't take off. He used to tell me I didn't have to worry."

A few notes scribbled in that notebook. What was in there? Then the older officer glanced at the younger one. What did that mean? "We won't take up any more of your time right now, Ma'am," Enders – that was his name – said. "But we may have more questions."
"All right, let me show you out." Leave. Just leave.

The four of them walked towards the front door. As they stepped outside, Enders said, "You have a nice garden."
"Thank you. Do you garden?"
"I don't have enough time to get serious about it. But I admire a nice garden."
"Really?" Lina said, "Rachel's just getting into it. She's never been much for gardening, but I told her it's so healthy. So good for you on a lot of levels."
"That's right," Rachel said. "Lina's been helping me a lot to get the garden ready for spring. Well, before Ron died, anyway."
"Oh, don't worry. We'll get back to it. In no time you'll be ready to put in the peppers and tomatoes. And the irises in the side garden will be coming up before you know it."
"That'll be nice."
"Look," Lina said, pointing towards one of the trees at the side of the house. "That's an apple tree. I made Rachel grow that from seeds. And now look at it!"
"Do you have apple trees too?" Enders asked her. Why did he have to do that? Now Lina would never shut up about her trees. Oh, well.

"I've got apple trees and cherry trees too. And I have a big flower garden. I'm thinking of starting a rose garden this year. Three different varieties."

"It sounds great," Enders said. "I'll bet you grow your own vegetables."

"Well, some of them. To be truthful I've not started with cucumbers or eggplant yet. But I'll get there. Right now, I'm just getting the perennials ready."

Rachel felt a throbbing pain behind her eyes. Why wouldn't everyone just be quiet and let her get back to sorting Ron's things? Who cared about tomatoes or cucumbers or peppers? Only a few more seconds and they'd be in the car. Then they would be gone. Then Rachel could sink into the quiet. The pain started again.

"Could I see the rest of your garden?" Enders asked. What choice did she have? "I guess so. If you'd like."

She took the police officers into the back yard. There wasn't much to see yet, but at least it looked clean. The two officers murmured some appreciative comments as they went. Lina didn't say much, thank God.

"Thank you for your time, Ma'am," Enders said, when they got back to the front of the house. Grant nodded his thanks and both officers thanked Lina and Rachel. At last they got in their car and shut the doors. There was a reassuring whir as the motor caught and the car pulled out of the driveway.

"I think I'm going to go in and lie down," Rachel said when they'd left.

"I don't blame you one bit. I can come back later," Lina agreed.

Good. She could get back to sorting Ron's clothes.

[108]

As the police car pulled away from Rachel's house, Luke said, "I didn't see any foxglove. Did you?" "Nope. Doesn't mean she couldn't have bought some, but she has none growing."

Six

"No, he didn't say anything to me," Emma said. "But let me look at his calendar again and see whether he had anything written in it."

While she looked up the calendar on her computer, Patricia made mental notes of what to focus on when they looked through Clemons' files. He had a neat office, so at least they wouldn't waste too much time wading through clutter. It was well-appointed too, as she'd expected. Solid teakwood furniture, simple but elegant small conference table and chairs, and a carpet in muted shades of brown, gray and beige.

Patricia didn't look behind her, but she knew Grant was watching her, still babysitting her while she interviewed. And that wasn't about to end any time soon. But still, he'd put her on interviews this afternoon and told Luke to follow up on Victor Wagner's story. And at least he didn't interrupt her. Besides, it wasn't as though she'd proven herself yet.

"Here it is." Emma's voice interrupted Patricia's thoughts. "No, there's nothing here. I didn't think he had any early meetings."

"Do you remember what time he got in that morning?"

"Well, I can't say for sure. But I think I'd have noticed if he got in a lot later or earlier than usual, and he didn't."

"And he usually got in at eight?"

"About that. It was unusual for him to get in any later than eight-thirty."

"That helps. Thanks. Is there anything else you can tell from that calendar – anything unusual?"

"Not really. He and I met, like I said, about eight, to go over his schedule. I gave him what he needed for his meeting with the gallery. He went over it for a little while and we had our morning meeting. After that he left."

"Do you remember if anyone came into his office while he was there?"

"Well, I know that nobody from outside the company did. I'd have noticed it. And, like I said, there were no early appointments that day."

"What about the people who work here?"

"I'm sorry, I couldn't tell you that. Ron – Mr. Clemons – had a kind of open door policy. People knew they could stop in to see him if he wasn't with someone else. Unless it was a client or someone else from the outside, I didn't keep track of who came in and out."

"That's fine. Do you remember if you were at your desk the whole time Mr. Clemons was in his office that morning?"

Emma thought for a minute. "I think I was. I mean, I might have gone to the ladies' room or something, but nothing else that I can remember. Nothing that would have taken me longer than five or ten minutes."

"Can you tell me about the morning meeting?"

"Oh, that. It was just our weekly staff meeting. It usually doesn't take longer than half an hour unless there's a problem."

"And who comes to those meetings?"

"Well, Trent Rakins does. So does Wade Messner, and usually so does Denise Bascomb. I do, too, to take notes. Other people come in once in a while to give reports, but those are the regulars."

"And he held that meeting that day?"

Emma looked at her computer screen again. "Yes, he did. It lasted the normal half hour that morning, so there must not have been anything unusual about it. I could get my notes from it if you want."

"That'd be great."

"I'm sorry, but I left them on my hard drive. I'll go print them off and be right back"

Emma got up from Clemons' dark-brown leather chair and left to go to her own office. When she'd gone, Patricia stood up and walked around the office to get a better sense of what she might want to look at more thoroughly.

Grant's voice reminded her that he was still there. "What's your take on what she said?"

Patricia turned around and returned to the seat she'd had. "First thought? Assistants at this level are usually smart and observant. That's what they're paid to be. The idea is to save your boss trouble."

"Go on."

"I'm just thinking that if something weird *had* happened that morning, it would have registered with her."

"OK."

Patricia was about to say something else when Emma returned.

"Here you are," Emma said, holding out a piece of paper. Patricia took it and skimmed through it. Then she handed it to Grant. Emma glanced at her watch and then towards the door.

"I know you need to get back to work. I'll look at these notes and then at the rest of the office, and let you know if I have any questions."

"That'd be fine," Emma said gratefully.

When she'd gone, Patricia got up again and this time sat down in Clemons' chair. Grant looked through the books and papers on the small set of shelves to the right of the desk. Emma had left the computer files unlocked so Patricia had no trouble opening and reading them. There wasn't much to see though. Mostly company profiles, financial reports and some copies of official correspondence. She spent a few minutes looking at the financial information she found, but there was nothing unusual about them. From what she could see, the company was doing reasonably well. Certainly, there wasn't any reason to be concerned for the company's future.

Then she went on to Clemons' business email. Nothing much there, either. Emma handled the company's correspondence, and Clemons would likely have kept anything personal in his personal email. She made a note to herself to look into that. She'd come to the conclusion that this guy didn't keep much of interest on his hard drive when Grant said, "Not much here. Just a few reports, some 'how to sell' books, and some company literature."

"I haven't found much either. All professional stuff here. Everybody's got something though. Do you think we should dig deeper? Get some computer people on this?"

"Not yet. We may need to do that at some point, but not right now."

They both looked up when Denise Bascomb walked into the office. "Oh," she said, "I didn't know anyone was here."

This time Grant took the lead. "Was there something you needed, Ms...?"

"Bascomb. Denise Bascomb. I'm a Client Rep. Who are you people?"

Patricia and Grant identified themselves. "I'm sorry to bother you," Denise said. "I came in to pick up a couple of books on selling that Ron – Mr. Clemons – offered me. I completely forgot about them when he passed away, and I'm finally getting to them now. I can come back later."

"Actually, we'd like to speak to you for a few minutes, if you'll just have a seat." Something in Grant's voice must have told this woman that she had no choice. She slowly sat down on one of the chairs in front of the desk. Patricia watched a little enviously. She'd have liked to have that air of silent command too. Maybe it was something you developed over time. She sat down, too, and waited until Grant gave her a slight nod.

"How long have you worked for the company, Ms. Bascomb?"

"Let's see, I suppose it's been ten years. Hard to believe," she said with a smile. Perfectly even, white teeth. Flawless makeup, too, and she made the simple ponytail she wore look elegant.

"And you've been a Client Representative for the entire time?"

"Well, for the first two years I was an assistant. Ron's assistant actually. Then I decided to try my hand at sales. It turned out to be the right choice."

"You and Mr. Clemons were friends?"

A quick flash of mistrust. "Not in the way you're probably implying. He helped me get my start. He's supported me here and I'll be honest, I've been good for the company, too. But we were friends and co-workers. That was all."

Patricia didn't want to blow this interview. Time to pour oil on the troubled waters. "Still, his death must have been hard on you."

"Oh, yes. It was horrible. I know his wife must be completely devastated, but it's been terrible for all of us."

Patricia paused a minute before the next question. How to put this the right way? "So, what are your plans now?"

"My plans?"

"Will you stay with Mid-Atlantic? Do you plan to move on?"

"Oh, I see what you mean." Good. No irritation. At least not yet. "I'll definitely stay here, at least for now. You see," Denise leaned forward slightly to make her point. "I understood the way Ron wanted this company to move forward. I shared his vision. I still do."

Keep treading lightly. Don't push things. Patricia leaned forward slightly too. "It sounds as though you're really loyal to Mid-Atlantic."

"Well, I am, you know. I feel I can really contribute around here. I know this sounds arrogant, but I am good at sales. I've been top earner for the Client Rep. team for the last couple of years. And I know where Ron wanted to take the company. I want to take it there too."

Something occurred to Patricia then. Something Luke had mentioned after his interview with Wade Messner. "I guess not everyone shares that vision?"

Bingo! Denise lowered her eyes and then said, "Let's just say we can't all agree on everything. Some people would rather the company, well, change its image. I think the image we have is a good one. That's all. And Ron agreed with me."

"So, you see yourself as a kind of heir to that vision?"

"You know, that's not a bad way of putting it. I know it probably sounds corny, but I really do want to carry on what Ron started. We have great clients and we can get more. We have a solid business plan and a golden reputation. I don't want to risk any of that. That's why…."

Grant telegraphed with his eyes: keep quiet. Let her talk. And he was right. Most people didn't like a lot of silence. If you sat and waited, they'd talk. Patricia sat quietly. Finally, Denise took a breath and went on. "That's been a source of friction, to be honest, between me and Trent Rakins. Have you spoken with him yet? He's Head of Client Services. You really ought to speak to him."

"Your boss?"

"Technically speaking, yes, but honestly, it's just nominal. Any of us could talk to Ron if we wanted."

"So, you and Mr. Rakins disagreed about the direction the company ought to take?"

"Yes, we did. He wants to go for, let's say, a different kind of client. Not the kind we've aimed for in the past. He thinks that he's the best one to lead the company, and he's sure that going for the, well, the middle market client is the way to move us ahead. He's wrong." Then she suddenly seemed to realize how much she'd said. "But that doesn't really have anything to do with Ron's death does it?

[116]

I mean, Trent and I disagree, but that's just one of those company skirmishes."

"I understand," Patricia said. "Did Mr. Clemons know how you felt?"

"Well, it was no secret, if that's what you mean. And it wasn't any secret that he didn't like Trent's ideas at all. He wanted us to be a high-end company. He even told me that he saw me as the one to move us ahead when he was ready to step down."

Don't pounce. Don't pounce. "He must have trusted you." A nod from Grant. Good, that was the right way to go about it.

"Oh, he did." A pointed glance at her elegant gold watch.

"I know you must be busy. Let me just ask you a few more questions and then I'll be out of your way."

"All right."

"Did you see Mr. Clemons on the morning he died?"

"For a bit. We had our weekly staff meeting. But I didn't really speak to him. I mean, not separately from the meeting."

"And he seemed his normal self?"

"Oh, absolutely. He was all excited about the gallery." A sad smile.

"And was everyone at that meeting"

"I think so. I was, Emma was, Ron was, Trent was there and so was Wade. Yes, I think we were all there."

"And after the meeting?"

"Well, we all left. I went to my office and didn't come out again until we heard the news."

Patricia made a few notes. "I think I have all we need for right now, Ms. Bascomb. You've been very helpful."

"Anything I can do, of course."

After Denise had left, Grant and Patricia looked at each other. "Ambitious," Grant said.

"Sure is," Patricia nodded. "Maybe enough to kill?"

"Could be. She's awfully careful though. Might not be willing to risk it."

"What's your take on what she said about Rakins?"

"The truth? Hiss, hiss," Grant made a claw-like motion with his right hand. "She's ambitious and she sees him as being in her way. Might not like him personally either."

"But we still talk to him again, right?"

"Hell, yeah, we do. He and Clemons had a strong and obvious difference in the way this company should be run. And Rakins is more or less second-in-command around here."

Rakins was at his desk when they got to his office. He looked up and quickly hid his irritation behind a wide smile. He rose and walked around from behind his desk, extending a hand as he did.

"Hello, Sergeant Grant. Nice to see you again. And you are...?" He looked appreciatively at Patricia.

"I'm Officer Stanley. Do you have a few minutes?"

"Why sure, I do. Come on in." He stepped aside, and they went in and took seats.

"Now, how can I help you? Are you making any progress?"

"We'd like to ask you a few questions. We're hoping you can help us clear up a few things."

"Glad to." Bonded teeth and nice smile, but he kept shifting one of his feet, and neither cop had missed his first reaction to their arrival.

"Thanks. How long have you been with the company?"

"Um, it's been almost fifteen years. I started as a Client Rep."

"And now you're..." Patricia looked down at her notes, but Rakins spoke before she could find the information.

"Head of Client Services. Anything to do with our clients, whether it's finding them, selling to them or getting them to pay, is my responsibility."

"So, you worked closely with Mr. Clemons?"

"I sure did. He depended on me when it came to our clients. And he trusted me to choose the best Client Reps and other client support people."

"Did you know him outside of work?"

"Not as well, I'll be honest. I mean, we had drinks together now and then, went to a couple of trade shows and conferences, that kind of thing. But mostly we talked business."

"Now, you said you didn't see Mr. Clemons the day he died, is that right?"

"Right, I was on my way to see a client. I do that sometimes, just to keep my hand in."

"So, you weren't at the morning staff meeting that day?"

'No, I wasn't.'

Patricia thought for a moment. Then she leaned slightly closer to Rakins. "I'm wondering if I can ask you a few questions about the business."

"Of course." Rakins smiled again.

"From what I've been hearing, Mr. Clemons saw Mid-Atlantic as staying mostly with, well, high-end clients. Am I right?"

"Yes, that was his idea," Rakins said. He couldn't quite disguise the contempt in his voice. "He wanted to stay with our exclusive clients – you know, only the *crème de la crème*." Patricia wondered whether he was going to roll his eyes. No, he controlled himself.

"And you shared that view?"

"Well, to tell you the truth, no. Don't get me wrong. Ron was a solid businessman. He understood his clients' needs, there's no doubt about that. But, well, you need to understand the way the market works. I thought he was missing out on a lot of potential growth by not expanding our reach."

"So, you thought it would be better to go for other kinds of clients?"

"Exactly." He said it in the same tone of voice a kindergarten teacher might use to praise a student. "I thought we ought to go for, well, a more diverse clientele. Still do."

"And is that your plan for the company now?"

"The way I see it, we need to get a wider base of clients. And that means going beyond our current reach."

"How did Mr. Clemons react to your views?"

"Well, he wasn't thrilled, I'll be honest. But I'm sure that with time, he'd have seen that I'm right."

"You argued about it?" Patricia could almost see the wheels turning in his mind. They must have argued. He had too strong a personality not to push his point of view. He was just trying to remember if anyone might have heard them. Finally, he answered.

"We disagreed, yes. Ron, well, didn't always like to consider other people's points of view. But as I say, I did respect him. He built this business up."

Patricia had been waiting for that kind of opening. "And now that he's dead, what do you see for the company's future?"

"I'd like to see us go after more diverse clients. I really want us to go for the middle market. There's such a lot of potential there."

"It sounds as though you've got solid plans for leading the company." Was he really going to go for that?

"Well, yes, as a matter of fact. I think I can take the company in the right direction."

Amazing how easily people said things when their egos were being stroked.

"And your colleagues agree with you?"

"Well, no two people agree on everything. I'm sure you know that."

"Oh, of course. It's always hard to reach consensus. But in general, your co-workers are behind you?"

"Well, not a hundred percent." A little self-deprecating laugh.

"Anyone in particular disagree with you?"

"Look, I don't want to tell tales out of school. We all work hard, and my colleagues are good people. Nothing against any of them. A crackerjack team."

"But...."

"To be honest, I think some of our people have a different idea about who ought to lead us."

"Who else is being considered?"

"A few people think Denise Bascomb is the right choice. And I agree she's smart and hard-working. But between you and me, well, she has some things to learn, that's all. She's not quite ready."

"Has she expressed interest in leading the company?"

A long moment passed. "As a matter of fact, she has. She's, well, she's got plans. She's ambitious. And maybe someday she can lead a company. But she's not willing to wait and be patient. Some people are like that and she's one of them."

"That's good to know," Patricia said. "Now, we won't take up any more of your –"

"In fact," Rakins interrupted her. "If you're looking – purely hypothetically, I'm saying – for someone who would have wanted Ron Clemons out of the way, I'd say Denise Bascomb might not be a bad place to start."

Patricia and Grant left Rakins' office after thanking him for his time. As soon as they were out of his sight, Grant rolled his eyes. "I'm surprised his ego fits in the car with him," he muttered. Patricia had to smother a laugh as they walked past the receptionist.

By that time, Patricia was beginning to feel hungry. She wasn't sure if she should say anything, but Grant made it easy for her (how did he know?). "Let's grab some sandwiches or something on the way back. Might even get something for Enders if he's been a good boy."

"Sounds good. I just want to pick up some copies of records that I thought we might want."

"What records did you ask for?'"

Did I remember all of the important records? What if I forgot something? Maybe I shouldn't have asked for any records at all without checking first. It was always these kinds of questions from her boss that made Patricia nervous. It wasn't that Grant was overly intimidating. And he didn't really lose his temper easily. That was probably why he was the one working with her and with Luke while they were still new at what they were doing. But even though Grant wasn't all that difficult to work with, she still didn't want to look like an idiot. And he'd be the one to do her eval at the end of the year. Besides, she didn't want to screw up the investigation. There was only one thing to do. When they'd first met, Grant had told her, "You're going to make mistakes. I can handle that. But I will not accept lies. Whatever happens, I want to know the truth." So, she took him at his word.

"I thought it would be a good idea to get some sales reports. I figured it might help us see how well the company's been doing. And I thought we should look at some accounting things too. You know, bills paid, bills owed, that kind of thing."

"Good idea," Grant nodded. "You can go over them after we eat." Yes!

When they got back to the station, Patricia dropped a hoagie, a bag of chips and a bottle of water off at Luke's desk. He was on the phone, but he waved at her and signaled his thanks. She took her own lunch to her desk and got started looking at the copies of sales and accounting reports she'd been given.

Most of it was routine, even boring. But as she looked over the sales data, Patricia saw one thing clearly. Denise Bascomb hadn't been exaggerating about her sales performance. She had the highest numbers of anyone on the Client Rep team, and not just for one quarter. Her sales performance was consistently at the top of the list. It might not mean anything as far as the investigation went, but it explained at least part of her rationale for wanting to take the reins. She certainly seemed to have the skills to bring in clients and get them to pay top dollar for Mid-Atlantic's services. So far, so good. The sales data showed the kind of company she'd thought it would.

Now it was time for the accounting figures, and that, she knew, would take longer. Payroll seemed all right. Everyone was listed as identified, and the salaries were what you'd expect. A little on the high side, but this was a high-end company that wanted to attract high-end people, so that wasn't too surprising. All of the other personnel numbers looked about right too.

Then she began to look at the records of client payments. The same clients were listed, which made sense. But somehow, something didn't seem right. It was hard to tell, especially given that Patricia didn't have an accountancy background. But something struck her as not quite what it should be. Something didn't match somehow. She decided to go over everything again to see if she'd made some kind of mistake. It was frustrating. It was right there, but she was having trouble seeing it. Maybe a walk and a bottle of water would help. Too much time staring at the same thing could make you see things that weren't there or miss things that were.

Fifteen minutes and one trip to the ladies' room later. she was back at her desk. Her shoulders and back were stiff from bending over the records even though she'd gotten up for a bit. But she took a sip of water and started again. There had to be something there. Wait! There it was! It *had* been there all along. A jolt of energy shot through her as she started circling numbers on client reports, sales data and accounting reports. Twenty minutes later she got up, stretched and picked up the papers. "Could you look at something with me?" she said to Luke.

"You've got something, don't you?"

"Not sure, but I think so. See what you come up with." She passed the sheets over to her partner and checked her work email while he read them.

A low whistle from Luke's desk told her she wasn't crazy. She looked over at him. "Did you see it?"

"Depends what you mean by 'it,' but I found some numbers that don't add up."

"That's what I thought too! It looks like the sales numbers that get turned in to the accounting people aren't the same as the client payments and other numbers that go on the other reports and they don't equal what's been deposited in the company's accounts."

"Exactly! Those are the differences I saw, too. Do you think it's just one sales rep playing with numbers, or do you think one of the accounting people has been changing numbers?"

"Hard to tell by just eyeballing it. But my guess is that the sales people have more to gain by artificially high numbers than the accountants do. Their pay isn't affected by sales data."

Patricia nodded. Luke was making a lot of sense. "Yeah, I can see that," she said slowly. "And as I think about it, there's one sales rep in particular who always seems to have awfully good sales numbers."

They looked at each other. "Denise Bascomb," they said at the same time.

They laughed a little and then Patricia said, "The only problem is, she couldn't get access to the accounting records. So she couldn't make any changes on their books. At least, not without calling attention to herself. But everything matches on the in-house records for sales data and accounting. The only thing that's different is what's actually billed to the client and deposited."

"She'd need some help from someone in accounting," Luke said. Patricia agreed with him. "If she had that though, it would be a good plan. Nobody's going to pay much attention to what the deposits say versus what the sales reports say except someone in accounting. And if someone there's in on it, it's an effective way to make a sales rep look good."

Luke was silent for a minute.

"What?' Patricia asked. 'Was it something I said?"

"No, no, it's not that at all. It's just that while you were looking at those numbers, I was looking over the Clemons family's personal finances." He went back over to his desk, picked up some papers and handed them to Patricia. She took them and looked them over.

"Well, their joint accounts look normal, at least on the surface."

"That's what I thought, too. Nothing there. But look at this." He pointed to the sheets of paper he'd handed her.

"Huh…Rachel Clemson's business account…" Patricia looked up. "It doesn't look so good."

"No, it doesn't. It looks as though she really needed a cash infusion."

"You think that's a motive?"

"Could be. I mean, she's about to inherit a lot of money. It might be just what she was looking for."

"Maybe. People have killed for a lot less money than that. She doesn't strike me as the type, but then, I don't know if there is a type."

"I think it's time to go show what we have to the boss."

Seven

Rachel turned around and went back into the house. They'd told her they didn't have any more questions, but they came back anyway. We'd like to ask you about your business, Mrs. Clemons. We understand you were having some financial difficulties. Oh, yes of course, with the economy the way it's been, all sorts of businesses have been taking a hit. More platitudes designed to put her off-guard. Why didn't they just come out and say it? We suspect you of killing your husband, Mrs. Clemons. Wasn't it always the wife or husband?

But that was their strategy. Try to put you off your guard. If you were too sharp for that, then rattle you by not accusing you, by making you wait for the shoe to drop. That had to be what they were doing. It had to be. How stupid can they think people are, to fall for that? But it's not going to work. No rattled nerves.

She looked up. It was a sunny day and starting to get warm. A good day to work on the garden. Yes, too much time in the house isn't any good. That's what people had been saying to her since the memorial service. Rachel, you need to get outside. Find a hobby. Well, she'd start today and do some work outdoors. She went into the tool shed Ron had put up behind the house. She got out the garden spade and fork that Lina had given her for her last birthday. That would be enough to get a good start. She took the tools to the garden at the side of the house and laid the fork down in the grass beside the weed-choked patch of ground where she'd once grown irises. Beautiful deep-purple-and-gold irises that didn't need much attention. That had been several years ago though, and the weeds had taken over as she'd gotten more involved in her business. Well, that was all right. She wanted a change anyway. Lilacs maybe, or something completely different, like geraniums or marigolds. Maybe even some sort of mix. As long as they didn't need a lot of attention; that was the main thing. She wasn't exactly a gardening pro and the police had been right about one thing. Her business needed some help and her time.

Damned police! Now she took her anger out on the soil, breaking it up into chunks as she went. *Thump, thump, thump.* Her jeans got earth stains on them and she knew she'd get blisters. But it didn't matter. There was something elemental, something cathartic about tearing up the soil. Yes, probably geraniums, pink and red ones. And maybe some petunias too. That would look nice and probably not require a whole lot of expertise. She'd go to the garden supply store tomorrow and see what they had. Now she brushed a lock of hair out of her face and got back to work. She felt some of the earth on her hands sprinkle onto her hair. Gardening gloves! She'd need those too.

Emma Yeats hung up the phone and looked at the pile of envelopes and papers on the desk in front of her. She wasn't a nosy person by nature; you couldn't be if you were in her position. But it was hard to resist the urge to go through those papers thoroughly. Ron Clemons had been a private person. Never rude, but certainly not forthcoming about anything personal. She wondered idly whether there was anything really interesting in those envelopes. No, it really wouldn't be professional. Besides, none of it was her business. She'd done the right thing by calling Ron's wife. Leave it all to her and let her sort through them.

She glanced at her watch. Five minutes to five; good enough. She pulled her purse out of her desk drawer, turned off her computer, picked up the stack of mail and got ready to leave the office. Mrs. Clemons (it felt strange to call her Rachel for some reason) had said it would be fine to drop it all by on her way home. Emma had only been to the Clemons home a few times, for company picnics, but she remembered how to get there.

Fifteen minutes later (no thanks, I really can't stay), she was back in her car and headed home. Mrs. Clemons was a nice enough person, but it felt awkward to talk to her and besides, Geoff would be waiting at the restaurant.

Rachel watched Emma's car pull away. Nice girl, and not bad-looking. She didn't think Ron had strayed, but she still felt glad that Emma was married. She dropped the envelopes Emma had given her on the living room coffee table and sat down to go through them. Some catalogues, a couple of journals, and a few trade organization letters. But what was that? A letter from a medical laboratory? What the hell?

She pulled the papers out of the envelope and read them, her face getting paler as she went on. Then she dropped the envelope and its contents onto the sofa beside her. She stared across the room for a long time. Then she picked up her phone from the coffee table where she'd laid it beside the mail. "Hello?"

"Lina, it's me. I – could you come over, please?"

"Honey, what's wrong? You sound horrible!"

"It's – could you just come over? I'll tell you when you get here."

"I'm on my way."

True to her word, Lina got to the house within half an hour. Rachel was still sitting on the living room sofa. Lina took one look at her face and sat down next to her. "What is it? Come on, I'm here. Tell me."

"It's this." Rachel passed the papers from the medical lab to her sister. Lina looked it over and put it back in the envelope. "Oh, my God," she said softly.

"Lina, what am I going to do?" Rachel swallowed hard.

"Do? You're not going to do anything!"

"I can't just do nothing about this, Lina. Ron has a son out there I've never met. Jason has a half-brother. This DNA report proves it. I can't just let it go!"

"You have to. Look, this Victor Wagner, whoever he is, is an adult. He has his own life. He's not your son. You don't owe him anything."

"'But don't you think he deserves to know he has a half-brother? A sort-of-stepmother?"

"Rachel, you told me that more or less, you and Jason get everything Ron left. There's nothing for this other person. He's not in the will so you don't need to contact him. Like I said, you don't owe him

[131]

anything. Besides, he's never met you, has nothing in common with you."

"What about Jason?"

"What about him?"

"Shouldn't he know that he has a sibling? Well, a half-sibling?"

"Why? What good's that going to do him? Look, I didn't want to say this, but I'm going to have to. Don't take this the wrong way, but you don't know anything about this Victor Wagner. What if, well, what if he doesn't want any contact with you or Jason?"

"He must have wanted contact with Ron. Somehow one of them found the other and both of them agreed to the DNA test. So, he had to be willing to go at least that far."

"Fair enough. But he hasn't gotten in touch with you, has he?"

"No."

"You see? He wanted to verify paternity. Who the hell knows why? He got his answer if he got the same results Ron did. And that's all there is to it. Ron didn't say anything to you about all of this, did he?"

"No, of course not. Don't you think I'd have told you?"

"All right, you'd have told me. But I still don't think you should try to get in touch with this person. Rachel, look at it this way. Suppose he's after money? Maybe he thinks he's in Ron's will somehow. You and Ron were doing well financially. Maybe he thinks he's going to get a share. Maybe Ron even talked to him about it. If you contact him, you may be opening yourself up to a big fight over Ron's will. And you might end up

[132]

cheating Jason out of his share. Is that what you want?"

Rachel looked up at her sister. She leaned back, closed her eyes and opened them again. "No, it's not what I want. Of course I don't want to cheat Jason out of money, if that's what this is about."
"You see? Problem solved. Just leave it, Rachel. Just get rid of this whole thing. You want me to just tear these up?"
"No, don't do that." Rachel spoke with a sudden firmness. "I want to keep it all until I figure out what to do."
"What is there to figure out? I've already told you it's only going to cause trouble if you contact this guy."
"I know you're trying to help, Lina. I really do. But this is my decision. Let me think it over and let me work out how I'm going to handle it, OK?"
Rachel held out a hand and waited until Lina put the papers in it. Then she put the papers back in the envelope and dropped it on the table. "Come on now. Let's have a cup of coffee."

Half an hour later, Lina finished the last sip of her coffee, put the cup down on the saucer and said, "I really ought to go. Kyle'll be home by now, and I forgot to leave him a note."
"All right, I'll just put these cups in the sink."
"I forgot my purse. Hold on." Something about Lina's tone of voice sounded different, more alert. Rachel decided to follow her. Lina went into the living room picked up her purse and then leaned over the coffee table, reaching for the envelope from the lab.
"Lina! What are you doing?"

Lina straightened up quickly. "I told you. I'm just getting my purse."

"And I told you, I'll figure out what to do about that," she pointed at the envelope. "Really. I can deal with it, OK?"

"Fine," Lina raised both hands in surrender. "I'm only trying to save you from a bucketload of trouble, that's all."

"I'm a big girl now, Lina."

"Yeah, you are. I forget that sometimes, I guess. I'm sorry." Lina gave her a sheepish smile and put her purse strap over her shoulder. Rachel walked her back through the kitchen and saw her out the back door.

When she'd gone, Rachel went back to the living room and thoughtfully picked up the envelope from the lab again. She opened it and pulled out the papers. Wagner, Victor. Age. Birthdate…. It felt so strange. A part of Ron that she didn't even know existed.

Lina get into her car, glancing back once at Rachel's house. She really wished Rachel hadn't found out about Victor Wagner. It was going to make everything so much harder as Rachel moved on with her life. Maybe she should try to talk her sister into getting rid of that paperwork. But no, the quickest way to get Rachel's back up was to tell her to do something. Hopefully, she wouldn't do anything about it – at least not for now. It would have been so much better if she'd never learned about Ron's past, but that couldn't be helped. The best thing to do was just to drop the subject.

"I don't know what they want with me," said Greg Isaacson. He turned over in bed and faced Denise. "They called yesterday and told me they wanted to talk to me today. That's all they said. I have no idea what they want."

"I'm sure it's nothing. I mean, you didn't even know Ron, did you?" Denise asked, running a silky hand up and down his arm.

Greg gently moved her hand and sat up. "No, I didn't know Ron, other than to say, 'Hello,' to when we passed each other in the hall. He didn't come down to Accounting very much."

"You see? They probably just want to verify some record or other, that's all. Stop worrying."

"Yeah, you're probably right. It's just…"

"Just what?"

"Well, you know. Us."

"What about us? What do they care who you sleep with? Or who I sleep with? Ron didn't know about us anyway."

"I know that. But what if they find out about your records. I know you don't like to talk about it very much, but we have to figure out what to tell them."

"I know." Denise sat up, hugging the sheet to herself. "I've been thinking about that too, to be honest. But they aren't looking for sales records. They're looking for someone who didn't like Ron. I mean, hated him enough to kill him. And you certainly didn't."

"No,"

"So even if they do ask about records, it doesn't matter. You didn't really even know Ron."

Greg turned to Denise again. "Did Ron ever find out about those sales numbers?"

"Are you kidding? If he had known, don't you think I'd have been fired? And for sure he'd have fired you. And he didn't."

Visibly relieved, Greg said, "I suppose that's right."

"So. nothing to worry about." She glanced over Greg's shoulder at the clock on his nightstand. "We'd better get going."

Greg turned and looked at the clock. "Yeah, we'd better. I didn't realize it was that time already. You go first in the shower. I'll make coffee."

"Deal."

Greg watched as Denise got out of bed. Maybe she wasn't in her twenties any more, but regular workouts kept her in fine shape. He knew how stupid it was to have a relationship with someone at work, but Denise was irresistible. He had no illusions about her interest in him. He wasn't the most stunning-looking man in the world, and certainly not the richest. But Denise found him useful. And good in bed, so she told him. Hard to tell if that was true, but it didn't matter. She had this way of wrapping people around her finger. He could see why she was so good at sales.

Denise stood in the shower and let the hot water stream over her. She needed to think, and it was hard to do that with Greg right there next to her. He was a nice guy, but there were some things he wouldn't understand. He'd never been in sales. He didn't get the pressure. She'd told Ron how hard it had gotten. "That's no excuse," he'd said. "You can't just change numbers like that."

"But you've done sales, Ron. You know what it's like. It's a battle all the time. For every dollar."

"Of course I know that. But if you can't be honest with me, how can I trust you?"

It was a good thing Greg didn't know about that conversation. She almost nodded to herself as she thought about it. Yes, it was much better for him not to know. But that still left the question of what he'd say to those police people. They didn't seem stupid, so they'd probably put two and two together.

Maybe she'd go to the meeting with Greg, just to be sure. Yes, that's what she'd do.

With a sense of resolve, she got out of the shower and dried quickly. Once she was dressed and made up, she went to Greg's kitchen where he'd already put out coffee. She took a cup. "This is much better than a hotel," she said.

"Service with a smile."

"You know, I've been thinking. Maybe I could go to that police interview with you."

"Why would you do that? You don't know all the Accounting details they want."

"No, but, well, maybe it'd be better if I were there."

"What for?"

"Call it moral support if you want."

"Nah, you don't need to do that.' You have enough to do."

"I don't mind. Really."

"I can handle it."

"But if they ask you about the sales numbers, well, I ought to be there."

Greg thought for a minute. She did have a point about that. He was probably being manipulated, although he couldn't figure out what she wanted in this. But it did make some sense. And he couldn't see any harm in it. Besides, he knew Denise well enough to know that she wouldn't give up until she got her way. She wasn't shrewish or pouty, but she was persistent in her own way.

"All right," he finally said. "I guess there's no reason you shouldn't be there."

Denise smiled. It would all be fine now. She finished her coffee and placed the cup in the kitchen sink. "Time for me to go," she said. She kissed Greg and stroked his cheek with a thumb. "See you at the office."

"See you."

"Oh, what time did they say the interview is?"

"They'll be there at nine."

'Got it."

Denise glanced briefly up and down the street as she got into her car. It felt a little ridiculous to be so cautious about her relationship with Greg. But for right now it was probably best to keep it quiet. Especially with this whole murder thing going on. There'd be time enough to make it public when the cops were done interviewing everybody. If she and Greg got through this interview with no problems, that would be good enough for now.

"Come in. Please have a seat," Patricia said when the Head of Accounting arrived. She and Grant had gotten the use of the smaller of Mid-Atlantic's two conference rooms for interviews. They'd both figured it would be easier than having everyone come to the station, at least for the moment. Now she hoped her voice didn't sound as tentative to this accounting person – Greg Isaacson, his name was - as it did to her. Asking interview questions was hard

[138]

enough; learning to do it with the right tone of voice was even harder. You had to be in control, even in charge, without sounding bullying or confrontational. It wasn't easy to do well.

"I understand you wanted to speak to me?"

"Yes, that's right. As I'm sure you know, we're investigating the death of Ronald Clemons."

"I heard that, yes. I'm just not sure how I can help you. I didn't really know Mr. Clemons."

"You knew who he was, though."

"Well, yes, of course. I –"

The door to the conference room opened and Denise Bascomb came in. "I'm sorry to be late," she said a little breathlessly as she took a seat.

Grant's eyebrows were raised, and he'd moved a little out of his seat. So, he hadn't been expecting this either.

"I'm sorry, Ms. Bascomb. This is a private interview. I'm going to have to ask you to wait in your office or another room."

"But," Denise placed her purse determinedly on the table in front of her. "Greg and I decided that it would be better to speak to you together."

"I realize that, Ms. Bascomb, but we really need to speak to Mr. Isaacson privately right now. If you'd like to talk to us, maybe you could stop in after we're done here."

"But, well, there's something we should probably say to you together." Denise faltered a little. But she wasn't giving up ground entirely.

Let them stay together or not? She didn't dare look over at Grant and let these people see her as unsure of herself. She didn't want to lose Denise's cooperation. At the same time, there were good reasons not to keep them in the same room.

"Tell you what," she finally said. Here goes. "We'll speak to Mr. Isaacson now, and then when we're done we'll speak to you together."

"All right, I guess," Denise said, clearly not pleased about it. She slowly picked up her purse and left.

"Now, Mr. Isaacson, let's talk about these accounting figures." Patricia turned her attention back to Isaacson. He hadn't said a word while Denise Bascomb was in the room, but when she slid some papers across the table to him, he started to focus.

"What do you need to know?" he said in a small, tight voice.

"If you'll look at this information," Patricia pointed towards one of the forms. "You'll see that there's one set of numbers. Sales figures, client purchases, and so on. But if you look at these," She pushed another form slightly closer to Isaacson. "They don't show the same numbers. These numbers are bank deposit entries and payments from clients. Shouldn't those numbers match?"

"I'm not sure what you mean.'"

"For one thing, shouldn't the numbers from sales figures equal the amount of money that clients actually pay?"

"Well, usually they do. But sometimes, well…" Isaacson looked away and then back to the paper. "We may give some sort of final discount or something."

Patricia waited a minute. Rotten liars always liked to fill up silence with words if they could. She'd at least learned that much. Finally, Isaacson spoke.

"They're supposed to match, yes. I can't tell you
right this minute why they don't. I'd have to look
into it, see what happened."

"You know what else I noticed?" Patricia ploughed
ahead. "There's one sales rep whose stated sales
figures are consistently higher than what clients
actually pay. Denise Bascomb. Any reason why that
would be?"

"I'm not in sales," Isaacson faltered.

"No, but you are the one who's supposed to make
sure everything balances out. It doesn't though.
Why?" The merest shake of the head from Grant.
Don't push too hard. She backed off a bit. "What
might make these numbers different?"

"Well, like I said. A discount, a special 'thank you'
to a big client. Sometimes a courtesy if we couldn't
do exactly what the client wanted as quickly as they
wanted. I've heard of that kind of thing being
done."

"But so consistently by one rep?"

She looked steadily at Isaacson, who wouldn't look
back at her. "Look," she said, a little more gently,
"You're a lot better off telling us now than having
to tell us later."

Finally, Isaacson sighed. "All right. Denise – she
and I are together. She had a little trouble keeping
her numbers up, asked me to help. The deal was that
when things got better, I'd stop."

"And they haven't?"

"They're getting there. But I didn't kill anybody!"

"Nobody's saying you did. We're just trying to put
all the pieces together. You can help by telling me
how this worked."

And Isaacson did. Nobody'd noticed that the sales numbers didn't exactly equal the payments. And since he was Head of Accounting, it wouldn't have mattered anyway. It was only a little each time, not enough to get anyone's attention. "Besides," he explained. "Denise isn't greedy. Competitive yes. But not greedy."

After a few more questions, Isaacson left. They had all the evidence they'd need to prosecute him for financial crimes, but as Patricia told him, if he co-operated with the murder investigation, they would take that into account. He'd have a lot to think about.

"We need to speak to Denise Bascomb again," Patricia told Grant.

"Agreed. Let's get her in here. I don't want them to have time to talk."

Patricia nodded and left the conference room to look for her. She found Denise in her office.

"We're ready now if you'd like to speak to us," Patricia told her.

Denise took one look at her face and said, "Looks like I'd better."

"I think that would be a good idea."

Back in the conference room, Denise sat down, looked from Patricia to Grant and back again, and then said, "I know how this all must look. But I never stole from anyone. I never kept one penny – ever – that I reported as a sale. I'm a lot of things but I'm not a thief."

"So, tell us what did happen," Patricia said.

"You know how the economy's been these last few years. It's been harder than ever to make sales. And the clients I work with have been buying less. I'm out there all the time trying to get business, and it just hasn't been easy."

"Go on."

Denise absently twirled a ring around her finger. "I thought, well, I had to keep ahead of it all. Stay on top. If you don't, you're a dead duck in this business. You can't give an inch and you always have to look behind you. That's how it is. So, I had to do something." Her speech got a bit more rushed as she went on. "I decided the best thing to do would be to, well, make it look like my numbers were as good as ever. Like I was doing a great job. I figured I'd be safe that way."

"Safe?"

"Don't you get it? This is a vicious business. I mean, Ron was a good boss. He was good to work for, supportive, the whole thing. I had nothing against him. I liked his ideas and I thought he had good business sense. But that's just why I was afraid. If he'd known my numbers were dropping the way they were, he'd have had no choice but to cut me loose. And he'd have been right. You can't afford to keep anybody who's not bringing it in. Not in this game."

"Did he threaten to fire people who didn't bring in a lot of sales?"

Denise brushed back the platinum ponytail that had fallen over her shoulder. "No. He wasn't that explicit. And he wasn't looking for reasons to fire people. But he wasn't stupid. He knew how the economy was going. He'd have been good about it, but I'd still have been fired. And once you lose your job, it's really hard to get another one."

"So, you altered your sales figures."

Denise nodded as she took a sip from the bottle of water she'd brought with her. "Never by an awful

[143]

lot. That would have been obvious. And not always the same amount. But I just didn't see any other choice. And, well, there was Greg."

"How did he fit into it all?"

"Greg's Head of Accounting. Right, you know that. Anyway, he took the sales figures I gave him – the ones I fixed. Then he made sure the other sales records were consistent. The client payments and bank records weren't altered. It would have been too hard to do that without it being noticed. But since Greg's in charge of what happens in Accounting, he's really the only one who knows exactly how the sales and other records tally with the deposit and payment records. And he wanted to help me. He and I are together."

Patricia had been making notes while Denise was talking. Now she looked up and said, "Did Mr. Clemons ever find out what was going on?"

"No. At least, he never said anything to me about it if he did. And he would have. He might have talked to Greg, but I doubt it. He trusted Greg. And me."

"So, he didn't know about these records."

"I just told you, no." Then Denise straightened up, a little of her former confidence returning. "And that means I didn't kill him. I had no motive. As far as he was concerned, I was a valuable colleague. He liked me. I liked him. No motive."

"Is there anything else about this that we should know? The more you tell us now, the less we'll wonder about."

"I don't have anything more to say. I mean, there is nothing more. I changed the numbers, Greg made it all look good for Accounting, and that was it."

"All right. Please let us know" – Patricia slid one of her cards across the table to Denise – "if anything else occurs to you."

"I will." Denise put the card into her purse, got up, picked up the purse and water bottle and left.

When she'd gone, Patricia said to Grant, "You believe her?"

"Do you?"

"I don't know. Some of it, yeah. She probably did get desperate. The economy's been bad, even here. And I can see her working with Isaacson on those numbers. But I don't think she's telling the whole story."

"She's in sales. Her job is to make the product look good. This time the product is her. So yeah, she probably isn't telling everything. The problem is, we don't know what else she could be telling us. We'll just have to keep our eyes and ears open."

"You think we should talk to Isaacson again?" Patricia asked.

"Not right now. Let's let him think about it. Once it hits him that it's over for him here, he may have a few other ideas to share. For now, let's talk to the assistant again."

"Emma Yeats?"

"Yeah. She'll be in the best position to know if our guy was upset about anything. And I want to hear more about that staff meeting."

"I'll get her in here, then."

"Upset? No, I don't think so," Emma said. "I mean, he was focused on the Spenglar meeting, but he wasn't angry or upset. Maybe preoccupied, that's all."

[145]

"Did he say anything to you about what was on his mind?"

"Not more than usual. And we didn't have a lot of time to talk, anyway. We had a staff meeting and then he was off to the meeting with the Spenglar people."

"About that staff meeting," Patricia said. "Did anything unusual happen there?"

"Not that I can remember. Just the usual reports and so on."

"And everybody was there?"

"You asked me that before. They all were, honestly. I can't think of anyone who was absent."

"Just making sure. I know it's annoying to be asked the same questions again and again. Do you remember if Mr. Clemons talked to anyone after the meeting?"

"Not that I saw."

"What was he like when he left the building?"

"Rushed. Preoccupied, like I said. He didn't say much, but he did say he'd be back."

"Did he have any appointments in the afternoon?"

"Not with clients if that's what you mean."

"With anyone?"

"Wait a second," Emma's delicately arched eyebrows puckered a little as she thought. "I remember!" Her face cleared as she said, "He asked me to make some time for Denise Bascomb."

"Did he say why?"

"No, just to make sure to put it in the calendar."

"Did you tell Ms. Bascomb this?"

"You know what? I didn't! I mean, I was going to, but I didn't see her, and then by the time I did, we'd already heard the news. The whole thing completely slipped my mind."

[146]

"And you don't know what he wanted to see her about?"

"No," Emma shook her head. "Like I said, he just asked me to make some time for her, that's all."

"Can you remember whether he told you who wanted the meeting?"

"I'm not sure what you mean."

"Was it his idea to meet with her, or did he say she wanted a meeting, and ask you to schedule it?"

"Oh, I get it now. Let me think." Emma tapped an index finger on the table as she tried to remember. "He said he needed to speak with Denise, and to please make time for her. I can't be sure, but it sounds like it was his idea."

When Emma left, Grant and Patricia began to look over the notes they'd made from their interviews. After a few minutes, Grant said, "So, what do you think we've got?"

Patricia sometimes wished he wouldn't ask questions that way. It always sounded as though he were quizzing her. But acting like an insecure bundle of nerves wouldn't help anything. She looked down at the papers and said, "I'm also pretty certain that Denise Bascomb isn't telling the whole story."

Grant nodded. "I had the same idea."

"And," Patricia added with a little more confidence, "Something else just hit me. Something Emma Yeats said."

Grant raised his eyebrows.

"She's told us twice now that everyone was at that staff meeting on the morning Clemons was murdered."

"Right."

"But Trent Rakins told us," she flipped through her notebook, "that he went to an early meeting with a client and didn't make the staff meeting that morning. He says his assistant told him the news."

Grant leaned back a bit and raised his eyebrows a little further. "We might make a cop out of you yet, Stanley. Good catch. You think he's lying, or you think Emma Yeats is?"

"Could be one or the other made a mistake." Grant nodded, and she went on. "*If* it was a mistake it was probably more likely his than hers. Assistants are paid to notice and remember everything. She'd have mentioned it if he wasn't there, unless he specifically asked her not to. In which case I think we'd want to know why. But if it was just a slip-up, it seems to me he'd have been the one to maybe get the date wrong. His assistant probably keeps all of the records."

"And if it wasn't a mistake? If one of them's lying?"

"Still more likely him behind it all."

"You don't like him, do you?"

"No, not particularly, but that's not the point. If Emma Yeats is lying, it's probably to cover up for Rakins. I can't see she has anything to gain for herself by saying he was there if he wasn't. So either he asked her to lie, or paid her to lie, or, well…"

"…She's got a thing for him."

"Exactly. But I don't see it. Still, she could."

Privately, Patricia couldn't imagine anyone having an interest in Trent Rakins. He was far too self-important and condescending. But he was handsome in his way, and rich. And on the verge of taking over the company. That might be enough for someone.

She went on with her point. "Rakins has a lot more motivation to lie. He's about to take charge here. He wouldn't be in that position if Clemons were alive. Besides, he didn't like the way Clemons was running things. You put those things together, and it sounds like a motive to me."

"We need to talk to Rakins' assistant," Grant said. "Find out if there really was a client meeting that morning." Patricia made a note and Grant continued. "Then let's find out whether anyone saw Clemons eating or drinking anything at his office. The digitoxin got there somehow."

"Right.'"

Twenty minutes later, Patricia had her answers. Max Anselm told her that Rakins had nothing scheduled early that morning. In fact, he'd said something about going to the staff meeting. No, he hadn't said anything about meeting Clemons privately. Yes, he'd come back to his office from the staff meeting. No, Clemons hadn't come in to Rakins' office. No, he didn't know anything else.

Emma Yeats wasn't much more helpful. There sometimes were bagels or doughnuts at staff meetings. And usually she made a pot of coffee. But she couldn't be one hundred percent sure whether her boss had had either that morning. She'd been busy taking notes and besides, she wouldn't have been paying much attention to it one way or the other. The only thing she did know was that nobody else had felt ill that morning. To Patricia that meant that the digitoxin hadn't been in the coffee or food served at the meeting. It would've been awfully risky for anyone to poison one person's food or drink in a group setting like that. Still, you couldn't completely discount it.

When she told Grant what she'd learned, he said, "All right, let's narrow things down a little."
"OK. We have at least three people with a strong motive. There might be others, but we have three: Rakins, Bascomb and Isaacson. And all three have been lying to us."
"Fair enough. Keep going."
"And any of the three of them could have had access to Clemons the morning he died."
"In fact, he specifically wanted to talk to Bascomb."
"Right. And she's in a conference call right now. I'm going to ask her about that when she's through."
"Assuming she tells you the truth, we still have to put digitoxin in one of these people's possession. So first, find out what she tells you. Then we'll start looking at it from the digitoxin angle again. It's probably foxglove, so keep following up on that."

Patricia saw her boss' point of view. They would have to figure out how the poison fit in. As she returned to Denise Bascomb's office, she passed by the larger conference room – the one in which staff meetings were usually held. She went in and looked at the layout. It would have been hard for anyone to move around the room without being seen. And if the coffee were in a communal pot, and the food in just one box, there wasn't much chance of making sure that the digitoxin ended up in exactly the right cup or doughnut. The more she thought about it the

more unlikely it seemed. In the meantime, she did
want to talk to Denise.

When she got to Denise's office, she saw that the
phone conference was over. Denise waved her in.
She wanted to do this right. "I'm sorry to bother
you again. I just had one more question." Oh, God,
she sounded just like Columbo!
"Sure. Go ahead."
"On the morning he died, Mr. Clemons told his
assistant he wanted to meet with you that afternoon.
Did you know that?"
"Really? He did? No, I didn't know."
"Would you know why he might have wanted a
meeting?"
"I'm sorry, I've no idea. It could have been any one
of a million things. You'd have to ask Emma."
"Well, that's the thing. She said she didn't know."
"Hmm...that's odd. Usually Ron told her what a
meeting would be about. Sorry I can't help you."
Patricia thanked her and left, sure that she was
being lied to again.

Eight

Luke had news for Patricia and Grant when they got back to the station.

"We got the final tox report on Ronald Clemons," he told them. "Not much of a surprise, really." Patricia sat down at her desk, and Grant took his usual seat between her desk and Luke's. "So, enlighten us," she said.

"OK, these tests confirm what we've thought from the beginning – toxic levels of digitoxin. They couldn't tell me exactly how the poison was ingested, but one thing did come up. Digitoxin usually takes effect between half an hour and two hours. So, whatever our guy had that contained it, he likely had it between seven-thirty and nine or so that morning."

"Do you think that lets out the wife? She says he left home at seven-thirty."

"Possibly. Depends if he ate or drank anything at home, and when."

"Find that out, Enders," Grant put in.

Luke nodded and went on. "It also means it wasn't anyone at work unless he had something to eat or drink between eight-fifteen and nine."

"Can't be a hundred percent sure of that," Patricia said, "but we know he didn't have a breakfast meeting or anything obvious like that. The only thing he might have done is had a cup of coffee or something, but nobody saw it if he did."

"Besides," Luke said, "Say he did. He gets to the office at eight-fifteen, talks with his assistant, has the staff meeting, then he leaves. Right?"

"That's what they've told us."

"So, the earliest he'd have been able to get coffee would have been about eight-forty-five. You push it, it's eight thirty. But still, they're already in the staff meeting."

"And?"

"Didn't you just tell me nobody saw him have anything?"

"That's true. And if he'd been poisoned just as he left the meeting, there wouldn't have been time for it to take effect."

Grant had been listening quietly to this exchange. Now he spoke up. "Forty-five minutes. That's the time between when his wife says he left for work and when he meets up with his assistant. It takes maybe twenty minutes in traffic to get to his office. We need to focus more on anywhere he might have stopped on the way. Someplace that sells food and drink at that hour. Stanley, find out what's on the way to his office and talk to them."

Patricia decided that the best way to start would be to find an online map of the route. Then she'd narrow down the possible places. There was no guaranteeing that Clemons had taken any particular route on that morning, so she'd just have to go with the most likely one.

That 'most likely' route didn't include a long list of places to stop for coffee or breakfast. Patricia had narrowed it down to three strong possibilities. After showing her list to Grant, they'd decided that it was best to visit them in the morning at about the same time as Clemons might have been there. So now Patricia was standing at the local Starbucks nursing

[153]

the tall latte she'd ordered. As soon as the line of customers had been served, Patricia took a picture of Clemons out of her wallet and showed it to the baristas on duty. None of them recognized him, but that wasn't a guarantee that he couldn't have been there. It was a busy place.

When she finished her latte, she moved on to the next stop, Nudy's Café. This was part of a smaller, local chain that served breakfasts and lunches. The food smelled good, but Patricia decided to hold out, since she was meeting Becky for breakfast at her third stop. She did get a cup of decaffeinated coffee though.

"No, I'm sorry," said the server when Patricia showed her the photograph. "I work mornings all the time, and I don't remember seeing him. I mean, he might have come in once in a while, but he's not a regular. You want me to check and see if anyone else knows him?"

"That'd be great. Thanks."

"Be right back.'"

True to her word, the server returned in a moment or two with the two other servers on duty. No, sorry, neither of them knew the guy, either. Patricia thanked them, finished her coffee and left, making sure to leave a good tip.

Now it was time to meet Becky. It had actually been Becky's idea to meet at the last of the three stops Patricia had thought of as likely places, since they both liked it. The café was called A Taste of Home, and featured small round tables, basket-weave chairs and fresh-made warm rolls with butter. Not good for your health, but good for the soul. They had strong coffee, too, and four kinds of tea, which was Becky's preference. When Patricia got there, she saw Becky's navy-blue Hyundai in the parking lot. She parked next to it and went inside the café. She soon spotted Becky, who had already gotten them a table. Becky waved when she saw Patricia and within a few minutes they were looking over the menu.

"Well, I know I want to split an order of rolls for sure," she told Becky.

"Yeah, me, too. And I think I want a mushroom omelet."

"I'm just getting two scrambled eggs, I think. I'm going to fill up on the rolls," Patricia said with a grin.

"You'll get them out of my cold, dead hands," Becky said, laughing.

Patricia had planned to ask about Clemons right away but when the food arrived, she changed her mind quickly. It all looked and smelled too delicious to ignore. Besides, she'd promised herself not to put her work ahead of Becky. You have it too good with her, she reminded herself. The picture can wait.

After a few bites she asked, "How's the omelet?"

"Mmmph," Becky answered with a nod.

"I'll take that as a ringing endorsement."

Becky nodded again and swallowed. She took a sip of her tea and said, "How're the eggs?"

"They're great. I love the way they put just a hint of scallion and garlic in them. Perfect!"

The next few minutes were silent as the two ate. When she'd almost finished her omelet, Becky said, "So we're really here to find out some information, right?"

"I do want to ask a couple of questions. I promise it won't take a long time."

"That's OK. I need to go to the bathroom anyway."

Becky got up to head for the ladies' room and Patricia caught the eye of their server.

"Can I get you something more?" she asked when she got to the table.

Patricia thought about their cheese Danish pastries. "We'll probably pick up a couple of Danish pastries to take along. Actually, though, I have a few questions I'd like to ask you." Then she showed her police ID.

"Is – is something wrong?"

"I'd like to know if you remember seeing this man" – she showed Clemons' photograph – "here at the café."

The server held up the photograph and looked at carefully. "Yeah, I know that guy. Haven't seen him lately but he usually comes in once a week or so."

"Thanks." Then she looked at the name badge on the server's uniform. "Your name's Lucy?"

"Yeah. Lucy Westmark."

"OK, Lucy. Can you tell me anything about him?"

"Not much. Takes his coffee black. Sometimes he has breakfast, sometimes it's just coffee. He's a pretty good tipper." Now curiosity got the upper hand. "Did something happen to him? Did he do something?"

"Actually, we're investigating his death."

"Oh, my God! He was murdered?"

"We're looking into it now, and I'm very glad of your help. You say he came in here regularly?"

"Well, I mean, not every day, but, yeah, most weeks."

"Did you ever see him with anyone?"

"Sometimes. When he was, it was usually with people he worked with, I think. I don't know, but their conversation sounded like business. You know, clients or something like that."

"Did he ever seem upset? Anything unusual you noticed?"

"No, not really. It just looked like business stuff to me."

"Do you remember the last time he came in?"

"Let me think." A tap of fingers on the table. "I got it! Maybe about a week and a half ago, maybe a little longer than that."

"Do you remember the exact day?"

"Let me think. Wait! It was the 14th. I know that because I had to drop off my car for inspection."

The 14th. The day Clemons died.

"Can you tell me about that visit?"

"He came in, had some coffee. I know because I remember serving him. Didn't order any food."

"Was he with anyone?"

"Not when he came in, no. But," she said, with a conspiratorial look, "somebody did join him."

Patricia tried to avoid looking too eager. "Can you tell me about that person?"

Just then she saw Becky coming back from the bathroom. Becky paused when she saw Patricia sitting across the table from Lucy. Then she pulled her phone out of her purse. A few seconds later, Patricia's own phone buzzed against her hip. She said, "Excuse me just a second, please," and pulled out her phone.

Gotta go now. C U later. Love ya

[157]

Patricia nodded and smiled in Becky's direction.
Then she turned back to Lucy. "I'm sorry. Now,
let's talk about that person you saw with Mr.
Clemons."

"OK, well, it was a lady. Seemed to know him.
Called him 'Ron,' They hugged. They had a cup of
coffee. Talked for a little, and then she left. He did
too, but not at the same time. Paid cash."

"Did they stay long?"

"Not really. Maybe twenty minutes?'"

"Did you hear anything they said to each other?"

"No. I mean, I heard her say, 'Hi, Ron,' but nothing
else. It was our morning rush."

"Can you remember what this woman looked like?"

"A little taller than you. Kind of red-brown hair."

"Fat? Thin?"

"About average I'd say. Didn't look like she needed
to diet, if that's what you mean."

"Anything else you remember?"

"Not really," a shake of the head. "Sorry. Nothing
else really jumped out at me."

"That's fine. You've been really helpful.'"

"Look, I'm sorry, but I gotta go," Lucy jerked her
head at the other tables.

"No problem. Thanks for your help. Here's my
card. If you think of anything else that might help
us, please get in touch."

Lucy nodded, tucked the card in her pocket, and
hurried away.

Patricia got up and left a generous tip on the table.
Then she picked up the check and went to the front
counter to pay. As soon as she was finished, she
went back to her Honda. Becky's car was gone.
Patricia smiled a little ruefully and pulled her phone
out of her pocket again. Then she texted Becky:

[158]

Sorry! Witness Interrogation 101. See you later.
Love you!

She dropped her phone on the seat next to her and
headed towards the station. Somebody – a woman –
had had a cup of coffee with Clemons on the
morning he died. And he obviously knew whoever
it was. Patricia thought about the women she'd met
who knew Ronald Clemons. Emma Yeats had black
hair and Denise Bascomb was a blonde. It wasn't
her natural color, but it was definitely blonde.
Rachel Clemons. Of course! Stupid as hell not to
start with the wife. She was a little taller than
Patricia and she had chestnut hair. Clemons would
have greeted her in a friendly way too, assuming the
wife wasn't lying about their relationship. She
hadn't told them about that visit to the café, either.
Wait a minute! Don't jump to conclusions. For one
thing, there's no evidence it was actually Rachel
Clemons, and she'd gotten pissed off enough the
last time she felt accused. And even if it was, that
doesn't mean she poisoned her husband. But
Patricia couldn't help mentally hugging herself a
little. Something felt right about this. There was
definitely a piece of the puzzle there.

When she got back to the station, Patricia was
disappointed to find that neither Grant nor Luke was
there. Grant had gone to an administrators' meeting
and Luke was at the department's sexual
harassment awareness seminar. She'd had her turn
three weeks ago and she knew Luke would be gone
for at least a couple of hours. She really wanted to
confront Rachel Clemons, but Grant had made it

clear he didn't want her interviewing any of the major people involved in this case unless he was there. Just one phone call couldn't hurt, though, could it? She eyed her phone for a moment and then reluctantly decided it wouldn't be a good idea. There were plenty of other things to do anyway. One of them was to check with local garden supply stores and nurseries to see if anyone had bought foxglove in the last few months. It was a long shot, but Patricia wanted to do something on the case and besides, you never knew. She wasn't a gardener herself, so she wasn't sure where to start. Oh, well, when in doubt, do an Internet search.

Ten minutes later, she had addresses for the three main local garden supply stores and the two nearest home improvement stores. She'd start there. Then there were the florists, not to mention the grocery stores that sold flowers. To Patricia it felt like a lot of wasted time, but she knew Grant would want her to be thorough.

By the time Luke got back, Patricia was exhausted and frustrated.
"What's the matter?" he asked as he sat down at his desk.
"I've spent the last two hours trying to find out if anyone's been selling foxglove plants."
"No luck?"
"The problem is that a lot of people buy it for their gardens and yards. Nobody wants to go back through their records for the past few months to look for particular names of customers. And even if they did, it might not prove anything. Whoever poisoned our guy could have had foxglove in their back yard for years. Or could have bought it at a

florist, or ordered it online, or God knows what else."

"Maybe that's the long way around."

"Meaning?"

"Meaning we stay with finding out who Clemons saw that morning during that hour or whatever. We narrow it down to, say, two or three people. Then we see if they have easy access to foxglove or to medical digitoxin."

"That's what I thought too. But I wanted to cover all the bases."

Luke looked down at the long string of X's on the list of telephone numbers Patricia had printed out. "Looks like you have."

Patricia leaned forward in her chair and stretched her arms. "When's Grant back?" she asked.

"Any time now. He said he'd be done about the time I was."

"Good. I've got news for both of you, but I only want to tell the story once."

Luke was right. Grant came into the office ten minutes later. He sat down with Luke and Patricia and said, "All right, somebody give me some good news. I've been in a waste-of-time meeting for the last two hours and I could use a break."

"I've got something," Patricia said. Luke and Grant turned their chairs towards her, and Grant said, "Shoot."

Patricia told them about her visit to A Taste of Home and about what she'd learned there. She finished up with, "And Rachel Clemons is the right height, with the same color hair. Doesn't necessarily mean anything, but if not, why didn't she tell us about it?"

[161]

Grant was silent for a moment. Then he said, "I agree. Let's talk to her again. Let's ask her to stop in this time. Stanley, you'll be with me. I'll ask the questions though. You got it?" Patricia got it.

They got hold of Rachel an hour later, and she agreed to come right over to the station. When she got there, Grant met her and took her into one of the interview rooms. Patricia joined them a moment later.

"I don't want *her* here," Rachel said curtly.

"I'll be asking the questions, Mrs. Clemons. Officer Stanley is only here to observe."

Rachel gave Patricia a scathing look but sat down and faced Grant. "You said you needed to speak to me again."

"That's right. We have a few more questions about the morning your husband died."

"I've already told you. He left home at seven-thirty. I never saw him again. Well, not until – until after they called me."

"You're sure you didn't see him?"

"Of course, I'm sure. Why are you asking me?"

Grant paused and then said, "A woman matching your description was seen meeting with Mr. Clemons at a local café just before he went to his office. We were wondering if that might have been you."

"It must have been a client or perhaps someone he knows from work. It wasn't me."

"We're fairly certain it wasn't a work colleague, Ma'am. That's why we wanted to talk to you."

"Then it was a client. Have you even talked to his clients?"

"We've been in touch, yes. But according to his schedule, he had no client meetings scheduled for that morning. His assistant told us he had nothing scheduled until the staff meeting that morning."

"Then I don't know who it was. It wasn't me, though."

"Can you tell us where you were that morning?" Rachel seemed a little more uncertain now. "I was at home until about nine-thirty, I guess. Then I went to pick up some dry cleaning. Then they called me from the hospital." "Did you call anyone? Send any emails?"

"I don't remember. I might have. I suppose you're going to check my records anyway."

"It's part of our routine, yes, Ma'am."

"I know you're supposed to always suspect the spouse. I suppose it's natural. I can't expect you to believe me, but I didn't kill Ron. I had no reason to want him dead."

Patricia wondered how Grant was going to manage this one. Would he mention Victor Wagner? Maybe this woman had no idea her husband had another son. Finally, Grant said, "There is the inheritance."

"You think I'd kill my husband for money?"

"We have to check everything, Ma'am."

"I know you're doing your job, but I didn't kill Ron. And I don't know who he was with that morning. I'm sorry that I can't help you, but I can't."

Rachel made it clear that that was all she was going to say. After a few more perfunctory questions, Grant finished the interview. Rachel stood up, nodded to Grant and glared at Patricia. Then she left.

Grant had seen the glare. Now he said, "You get used to it."

"I guess so. To be truthful, I'd probably glare at me, too." Patricia said a little ruefully. "So now we get the authorization to go through her phone and email records?"

"I'll get the wheel turning on that one."

Patricia was a little surprised at Grant's tone of voice. "I hope you don't mind me asking," she said, "but it sounds as though you're not sure about her."

He shook his head. "You learn not to trust anyone completely once you've done enough interviews. People lie. Or they forget things. Or they're covering up for something stupid but irrelevant that they've done. Or they're covering for someone else. So, you always check everything. But in this case, I'm inclined to believe her. I'll get the authorization, but I don't think we'll turn up anything, and I think we'll just alienate her more."

"Can I ask you one more question?"

"Of course."

"Why didn't you mention Victor Wagner to her?"

"Because we can't be sure whether she knows about him or not. If she doesn't, now's not the time to tell her. If she has found out, my guess is that something in her emails or phone call records will let us know. We'll ask her about it then. Unless we have to, let's not break his confidence."

Patricia privately agreed with her boss. She'd liked Wagner and although they still needed to check up on him, he didn't seem likely. And he had asked them specifically to keep their interview confidential. And yet, Rachel Clemons fit the description she'd been given of the woman who had coffee with Clemons on the morning he died. If it wasn't Rachel, who was it?

Rachel pulled away from the police station. Slowly, don't get a ticket here in the goddamned parking lot of the police station! They really did think she killed Ron. Now they were going to check phone records, emails, everything. It was like being naked in front of them. They probably knew about Ron's son, too. But if they did, why didn't they say anything? Of course! They were trying to make her feel comfortable – put her at her ease. They'd even arranged it so that other cop would ask the questions. Very clever. They were hoping she'd relax and tell them what they wanted to hear. They actually expected to coerce her into confessing to murder. Well, it wasn't going to work. They weren't going to get her to admit to anything. She nodded to herself as she made a mental note to call her lawyer. There was no way they would ever talk to her again without her lawyer.

She narrowly missed hitting the back of a pickup truck as she joined the traffic on the road. Pay attention! Worry about the lawyer when you get home. She thought about the phone in her purse. Usually she was glad of it but now it felt like another police officer sitting next to her, taking notes on her every facial expression. They were invading her privacy. There was nowhere to hide.

Nine

Three nights later, Victor Wagner left his office at the Chicago Stock Exchange to go home. It was six o'clock and he was already later than he'd told Syd he would be. And now that she was pregnant, she took these things really seriously. Well, if he was lucky, he'd make it home before seven-thirty.

It was nearly 40 miles to Palatine, where he and Syd lived – a long commute, but he'd heard of worse. And their house was in a good school district. They had to think about those things now. Besides, they couldn't afford anything really nice in Chicago itself. He was hoping that within the next year or two, he could start his own financial services business closer to home. But he had to finish his Certified Financial Planner courses and pass the test. And he had to hope that nothing would happen to their savings. Once the baby was born, Syd was planning to leave her job with the interior design company and spend a few years as a stay-at-home mom. "I can always go independent if I want to get back into it later," she said.

He smiled as he thought of how happy she'd been yesterday when their crib arrived. He'd spent an hour putting it together and setting it up in what would be the nursery. It would all be done ion green and yellow. "I don't want that sexist blue and pink crap," Syd insisted. And the room was really taking shape.

He brought his thoughts back to the road as he pulled into the traffic on LaSalle Avenue. It was bumper-to-bumper for a while, but it eased up once he got off Interstate 90. As he got closer to Palatine, Victor thought that he might actually make decent time.

The turn from Plum Grove Road onto Wood Street was always his signal that he was almost there. The traffic was much lighter now, and even though it was dark, it all felt homey. That was when he saw the car by the side of the road. A woman was standing next to it. He didn't want her to think he was going to hurt her, so he pulled close enough to be heard, but stayed in his car with the window rolled most of the way up.

"Ma'am, do you need help? Are you all right?"

"I'm so glad you stopped! Thank you. My car's stalled and my phone battery died, so I can't call for roadside assistance."

The words were out of Victor's mouth before he could think better of them. "Would you like to use my phone?"

She must have sensed his hesitation. "That would be great, if you don't mind. I promise – a two-minute phone call and I'll give it right back."

He smiled a little and handed her his phone through the partly-opened window.

He watched her as she paced around her car while she made the call. He always worried a little about stopping to help strangers. But there was nobody else in the car with her, and it wasn't as though this was a remote area. Still, he stayed in his car. It didn't make sense to make himself too vulnerable. As she'd promised, she was done in just a few

[167]

minutes and came over to the car to return the phone.

"Thank you so much. They should be here in about half an hour."

"That's great. You're lucky it's not raining."

"You got that right." She hesitated for a minute. "Listen, I was going across to that coffee shop when you pulled over. I still want a cup of coffee. Can I bring you back one? It's the least I can do after you saved my life."

"Sure, thanks. Just a small coffee would be great.'"

"OK, be right back." She walked across the street and soon disappeared inside the shop. While he waited, Victor called Syd to let her know what had happened and tell her that he'd be home in a few minutes. He had just finished his call when his coffee arrived.

"Here you go. I wasn't sure if you take anything in your coffee, so I just brought a cream and a sugar."

"That's fine. And thanks."

"No, thank *you*. I'm going to be fine now if you want to get wherever you were going."

"Sure?"

"Yeah, there are people around and the truck should be here soon."

"All right. Good luck."

"Thanks." She smiled as he pulled away.

A few minutes later Victor pulled into his driveway. He hoped the woman with the stalled car would be OK. She faded from his mind, though, when he went inside.

"Guess what came today," Syd said after she'd greeted him.

"What?"

"The rocking chair! It looks great with the crib."
She patted her swollen belly. "I can't wait for him
to see it." She took his hand and led him into the
nursery. She was right; the chair did look great.
"The baby'll love it." He kissed Syd and then
walked into the kitchen to heat up some food.
"I left you some casserole," she called.
"Found it!"
He heated up the casserole in the microwave and
joined Syd in the living room when the food was
ready. "Want some?" he asked.
"No, I ate, thanks."

They watched TV for about half an hour. That was
when the pain began. At first it didn't feel like
much. A little nausea, that was all. But it quickly
got worse. Now his chest started to hurt, as though
it was in a clamp. He gasped a little.
"What's wrong, hon?" Syd asked.
"I don't know. I feel awful!"
"Oh, God, I hope it wasn't the casserole! I ate some
and I'm OK, but still."
He bolted from the living room and ran for the
bathroom. A few minutes later he was back. "Syd,"
he gasped. "I really feel terrible and it's getting
worse." Then he slumped into a chair as the pain hit
again.
"I'm getting you to the hospital," she said sharply.
He didn't argue.

He didn't remember much about the drive. Mostly
he faded in and out of consciousness as the pain
ebbed and flowed. He felt hands lifting him and
then nothing for a while. Late that night he woke up
in a hospital bed. Syd was asleep in the chair next to
him. He reached out slowly and touched her hand,

which was resting on the bed. She slowly opened her eyes.

"Oh, thank God!" she said when she realized he was awake.

"What happened?"

"They said it was probably some kind of poison. They don't know what yet. They pumped your stomach and they're going to do tests. They said they want to keep you under observation until they know what it was."

He was too tired to say anything, so he squeezed her hand and closed his eyes.

The next time he opened them his room was flooded with light. Syd was still there, only this time she was awake, holding a cup of coffee.

"You're still here," he smiled.

"Of course I am!"

The door opened, and a nurse came in. "Good morning," she smiled. "You gave us quite a night last night, but everything looks much better this morning. The doctor will be in shortly to give you the dirty details. I just need to get your temperature and blood pressure first."

For the next few minutes the nurse got his vital signs and asked some questions. No, he wasn't in any pain at the moment. No, he didn't feel any nausea. Mostly he was just tired.

"The doctor'll be in in just a few minutes," she said as she left.

Ten minutes later the doctor paid him a visit. She looked over his chart and said, "How are you feeling?"

"Very tired, but that's about it. What happened?"

"We don't have the final report yet, but it looks like a very high dose of digitoxin. Your wife told us you don't have any heart conditions. Is that right?"

"No, I don't."

"And you're not on any medication?"

"No."

"Can you tell me exactly what you ate and drank yesterday, starting at about, say, six?"

He thought for a minute. "Just casserole. Syd had it too, didn't you, hon?"

"Yes, and I'm fine."

"No salads? No greenery?"

"No, I don't think so. The casserole was macaroni and cheese."

"Anything to drink?"

"A bottle of beer. But I opened it. It was sealed. Wait a minute!" It finally hit him. "You think I was deliberately poisoned?"

"Right now, I'm just trying to figure out how the digitoxin got into your system, that's all. I don't want there to be a next time."

Slightly relieved, Victor leaned back against his pillow. "Well, that's all I can think of. Can you think of anything, Syd?"

"No," she shook her head and took a sip of her coffee.

"I can't believe I almost forgot about it!" Both women turned to him. "It could have been the coffee!"

"Coffee?" the doctor asked sharply. She started making notes.

"Yes, I stopped to help someone whose car was stalled. She got me a cup of coffee at that place on Wood Street." Then he shook his head. "But that couldn't be it. I don't even know that woman.

Never saw her until last night. And I've had coffee there before – never had a problem."

"Well, we'll wait for the final report. I want you to rest today and we'll want you here overnight for observation. You had a very, very close call, I have to tell you. If your wife hadn't brought you in when she did, it could have been much worse."

Victor held Syd's hand as the doctor left. Why would anyone want to poison him?

Late that afternoon, Patricia hung up her office phone and stared straight ahead. Luke glanced over at her and said, "You look like a deer in the headlights. What happened?"

"You remember the boss asked me to get in touch with Victor Wagner?"

"Yeah, of course. He wanted you to nail down when Wagner left town."

"Exactly. Well, I just got off the phone with his wife. He's in the hospital – a case of poisoning."

"Poison?"

"Digitoxin poisoning."

Luke widened his eyes as the implication sank in. "Think it's the same person?"

"I don't think it's a coincidence if that's what you mean. They think it was in a cup of coffee. They found the empty cup in Wagner's car and they're testing it. They're testing some casserole he had, too. If the food comes out clean, at least we can be pretty sure his wife's in the clear. And if she is, then I think it probably is connected to our guy's death."

Luke thought for a minute. "Maybe he saw something or knows something? Someone got afraid."

"Possible, but he left town the morning after he talked to us. Since he knew we'd be interested in him, why wouldn't he tell us if he did see something?"

"Fair enough, but someone could still be afraid he saw something or remembered something or whatever."

"Maybe. If you're right, whoever it is could try again."

"We need to tell the boss about this. It might at least make sense to make a courtesy call to the police where Wagner lives."

Grant agreed. When they'd told him what happened, he said, "Probably a good idea. Stanley, get on the phone with – where's this guy from?"

"Palatine, Illinois."

"Get hold of them and tell them what happened and what's going on here. See what they want to do about it."

"He works in Chicago," Luke said. "You think we should tell them, too?"

Grant chewed his lower lip for a moment. "Not quite yet. They don't have jurisdiction in Palatine, where it happened. We can always get them involved later if we have to."

Two mornings later, Victor was watching the end of the morning news show on TV. He'd been released from the hospital, but he and Syd had decided it was best for him to take another day or two off from work. Truth be told, he was just as well pleased. The whole thing had taken a toll on him and he wasn't quite ready to face the world again yet. He was getting up to get some juice when he heard the doorbell ring. He went to the front door and looked through the peephole. On the other side was a woman holding up a police badge. He opened the door.

"May I help you?"

"Mr. Wagner?"

"Yes?"

"I'm Officer Drackmann, Palatine Police. I'd like to ask you a few questions, if you have a few minutes."

"Of course. Come in." He stepped back and Drackmann went inside.

"Please, come into the living room. Sorry it's a mess, but I've been home sick."

"It's fine. And actually, that's why I'm here. I'd like to talk to you about what happened."

"You mean about me being poisoned?"

"Yes, Sir. The hospital got in touch with us because it looks as though this poisoning wasn't an accident."

"I've been thinking about that. In fact, I was wondering whether I should talk to you myself, but first I was really sick, and then, well, I thought I might be imagining things."

"It doesn't look as though you were. From the test results we got from the hospital, it looks like you were given a large dose of digitoxin."

"Do they know how I got it?"

"The final tests aren't back yet. But just to be safe, we asked for a rush test on the casserole. We know there was no poison in that."

"You thought there might be? But Syd and I – we love each other! She'd never hurt me. I mean – why would she?"

"We have to look at all the possibilities."

"I know, I know. It just – it seems so impossible."
Victor ran a hand through his unkempt hair. "I
mean, who the hell would want to poison me? I
don't have any enemies. I'm not rich. I'm just a
finance guy."

Without directly answering the question,
Drackmann asked, "Can you tell me a little about
the woman who bought you the coffee?"

"That's where the poison was?"

"It looks that way."

"Well, she looked – I don't know, ordinary. It was
dark, so I didn't see her in full light, but she was
white, medium height, nothing special. Medium
build. Not dressed up, but not wearing jeans either.
Just pants."

"Young or older?"

"Older than me. I'm lousy at women's ages."

"Did you see what color her hair was?"

"Not really. It was cold, so she had a hat – one of
those knit hats – pulled over her ears. But I
remember that it was sort of light. I don't know,
maybe reddish-brown or something like that."

"That's fine. You're doing fine. Can you tell me
anything else about her?"

"Honestly no. She didn't have an accent or anything
you could really put your finger on."

"Glasses?"

"No."

"'OK, let's talk about the car. What was that like?"

"The car? Dark blue late-model Toyota four-door.
Maybe a Camry, something like that."

"You wouldn't be able to make my day and give me
a license plate number, would you?" she asked with
a slight smile.

"No," Victor shook his head a little sheepishly.
"Guess I noticed the car more than I did her. It had

out-of-state plates, but I don't remember which state."

"That's OK. You gave me a solid start. So, this woman used your phone?"

"Yes, she told me she needed to call for roadside assistance."

"Do you still have that phone?"

"Sure, it's right here." He reached into his pocket and pulled out his phone. He held it out to Drackmann, who quickly grabbed a tissue before taking it.

"Fingerprints! Of course!" he said.

"Yes, we'll check for those. If it's all right with you, we'll also check on the phone calls and other data on it. Something useful may turn up. Do I have your permission to check that information?"

"Yes, go ahead," Victor said, suddenly keenly aware of how much information there really is on a phone. He didn't like that invasion of his privacy. Sensing his reaction, Drackmann said, "I know it feels uncomfortable to have strangers looking at your data. But we might find something that will help us track down the person who poisoned you. It could be important."

He nodded. "I know," he finally said. "It does feel strange, but there's nothing really intimate on that. And I want to find out who did this, too."

"Thanks. You're making this a lot easier. OK, I think I've got everything I need for now. We'll be in touch if something comes up."

"All right." He got up slowly and walked with Drackmann to the front door. On an impulse, he said, "Do you think whoever did this is going to try again?"

She looked steadily back at him. "I won't lie, I don't know. But we are taking this seriously and we'll do our best to get you some answers. For now, take some extra precautions and call us if anyone you don't know tries to contact you, or if anything else happens."

"I will. And thanks."

She nodded and turned to leave. Then she suddenly turned back around. "Oh, and Mr. Wagner? Please tell your wife to take precautions too. Just to be on the safe side."

Then she was out the door and walking down to her car.

Syd! He hadn't even considered any danger to her!

Victor was waiting anxiously when Syd got home later that afternoon.

"Is something wrong?" she asked. "I've never seen you this jumpy."

"I got a visit from the police today. About the poison."

Syd sat down in one their homey kitchen chairs. "What did they have to say?"

Victor handed her a bottle of juice. "They found out that this whole thing really was poison. And they think it might be deliberate."

Syd's face drained of color. "Deliberate? But who? Why?"

"I don't know. I really don't."

She took a long gulp of her juice. "You think it might be some kind of weirdo? Maybe it was, well, random."

"I thought about that. And it might be. But there haven't been any other news stories about people getting poisoned around here."

"Well, what if you're the first one?"

"Maybe. But just to be safe, the cop told me that we should both take precautions, at least for now."

"Precautions? Do they think whoever it was is going try again?"

"If it's not a maniac of some kind."

Syd stared thoughtfully at her juice. "That means they think it might be someone who was targeting you."

"It might be."

"But why? That's the thing, Victor – why? You don't have any enemies. And it's not like we're rich or anything."

"Who knows? Maybe it is some sort of crazy person."

The sun was starting to set. Rays of it slanted in through the kitchen window and lighted up Syd's tawny hair. "Did they say we should go away for a while or something?" she asked.

"No, they didn't say anything about us going anywhere. They just said to take precautions."

She looked straight at him, trying to guess what he was thinking. "But you think we should? Go somewhere, I mean."

He looked down at the table, then up at her. His face looked drawn and his eyes anxious. "I'm scared as hell of something happening to you and the baby, Syd. That's what I think." Then with a rush, he stood up, stepped behind her and put a protective arm around her, his chin on her shoulder. "I couldn't stand it if anything happened to you."

She reached up and patted his arm, leaning her head against it. "I'm scared too. You should have seen how terrible you looked in the hospital. I thought we were going to lose you."

"Maybe we should go somewhere – just for a few days?"

"And let some whacko kick me out of my own home? No! I won't let whoever this is force me out of my house." Her hard tone of voice and the stubborn set to her mouth was all that Victor needed to know that his wife would not budge. He gave her a hug and then sat down across from her at the table.

"I don't want to give in to whoever this is either. But I don't want to put you and the baby at risk. Or me either, to be perfectly honest."

"So what do we do?" She reached out to hold his hand.

Victor sighed and straightened his shoulders. "Let's do this. Let's not go anywhere just at the moment. We'll be extra-careful about opening the door and answering our phones and emails. We'll touch bases with the police, and we'll see if they find anything out. If anything else happens, we'll go somewhere."

"All right." Syd nodded. "I guess I can live with that.' "

Rachel pulled into her driveway with a sense of accomplishment. She'd just finished delivering the last boxes of Ron's things to the local veterans' services charity. They'd find uses for his clothes, anyway. She'd already donated his selling and business books to the library, and the only other things left were his personal things like his wedding ring and the tie bar she'd bought him for their anniversary. She wasn't quite sure what to do about them. One step at a time. One decision at a time.

She got out of the car and walked back down the driveway to the mailbox. It felt odd to be the one getting the mail now. Ron had always been in charge of that. She opened the mailbox and pulled out the usual collection of ads and bills. Then she looked up from the mail just in time to see Lina's car pull in. She must have come from the opposite direction because Rachel hadn't seen her following behind. Lina parked and opened the car door. "Hi," she called as she stepped out.

Rachel waved. "I thought you were working today."

"Just got off."

Rachel looked at her watch. "Yes, I guess it is that time." She'd been hoping to have the entire afternoon and evening to herself, but apparently Lina had other ideas. I'm all grown up. I don't need a babysitter.

Lina must have noticed her expression. "What's wrong? Aren't you feeling well?"

"I'm fine. It's just that I wanted to get some things done, that's all."

"That's what I'm here for. Just let me know what needs doing and I'll do it."

"It's fine. I can manage. Really."

"I know you can." Oh, that tone of voice. As condescending as any pre-school teacher. "I'm here to lighten the load, that's all. Now, what needs doing?" There was no way Rachel was going to get rid of Lina, at least not for a while. Might as well give her something to do to make her feel useful. Lina followed her glance as she looked around the yard. "You're absolutely right! That hedge needs clipping. You've got a hedge trimmer, right?"

"I think Ron might have had one in the shed."

"I'll get going on it then." Thank God! Problem solved. The hedge really did need attention and it

would keep Lina busy long enough for Rachel to
get some things accomplished.

Rachel watched Lina go around the corner of the
house towards the shed. Then she turned around and
went inside. She dropped the mail on the coffee
table and went into the kitchen to make some tea.
The kettle hadn't even started to boil yet when she
heard the doorbell ring. She thought of letting Lina
take care of whoever was at the door, but no. Lina
already managed her life too much. She turned off
the kettle and went to the door herself. It was those
police officers again.
"Yes?" she asked. "What can I do for you,
Officers?" It was getting increasingly hard to be
polite to these people.
"We're sorry to bother you, Mrs. Clemons, but we
need to speak with you about an incident that
happened a few days ago."
This wasn't a courtesy call then. Better let them in.
They'd only come back again if she didn't. She
opened the door and gestured for them to come
inside. "What's this about?" she asked as they sat
down. It was the same two male officers who'd
come last time.
"Ma'am, have you done any traveling lately?"
"Traveling? You mean outside the country?"
"Anywhere, actually, in or out of the country."
"No, I've not been anywhere. Not even into
Philadelphia just lately."
"So, you've been in this area for the last few days?"
"Yes, I have. Why do you ask?"
"We wondered whether you might have gone to
Chicago."
"Chicago? Why would you think I'd go there? What
does Chicago have to do with anything?"

The two officers looked at each other. This time the older one, Grant, spoke. "Have you ever heard of a man named Victor Wagner?"

Rachel's face blanched. How could they know about Victor? Of course! If he and Ron had spoken at all, it would be in Ron's telephone records Say something, say something. She finally managed, "Who's Victor Wagner?"

She didn't fool either of the officers. Really, she hadn't expected she would. They were both silent for a short time, waiting for her to tell the truth. She waited, too. She'd learned enough from Ron and had had enough meetings with her own clients to know the value of just keeping quiet. Sometimes that was all it took to get the upper hand in a negotiation, or to keep it if you had it. It looked as though it was going to work this time too. The younger cop – his name was Enders, that was right – started to look a little restive.

He looked at his boss for guidance and then said, "You don't know anyone named Victor Wagner?"

"No, I'm sorry. I don't know anyone by that name."

They switched tactics. Using a 'let's be friends' tone of voice, Grant said, "To be honest, we'd be glad of your help. A few days ago, a Chicago man named Victor Wagner was poisoned."

"Is he still alive?"

"He'll be all right. We think this might be connected to your husband's death, and we're following it up."

"To Ron's death? You mean some crazy nut is going around poisoning people?"

'We're looking into all the possibilities right now."

"But what makes you think this poisoning has anything to do with Ron's – with what happened to Ron?"

Grant's tone changed, became more confidential. "Mrs. Clemons, this may be hard to hear, especially from a stranger, but Victor Wagner, the man who was poisoned, is your husband's son."

I can't do this any more. It's just too hard. Rachel dropped her eyes and drew a breath. In a quiet, but even voice she said, "I know."

"Did your husband ever talk to you about this?"

"No." She looked right into Grant's eyes. "I didn't find out until just a few days ago. I was going through some of his papers and found a report of the paternity test."

"And what did you do when you found out?"

"I didn't do anything. I mean, what was there to do?"

"You didn't try to contact Mr. Wagner?"

"What would I say to him? He's never even met me. It would have been too hard and too strange."

"Did Mr. Wagner ever try to contact you?"

"I don't think so. He never left a telephone message or sent a letter or email, if that's what you mean. I mean, not that I saw."

"She would have told me if he had," Lina's strident voice came into the living room two steps before she did. She was brushing her palms together as she walked in. "Rachel would have said something if this Victor Wagner had tried to call or visit. I mean, come on! You don't keep something like that to yourself, you know." Why did Lina always have to listen in? Her way of just taking over like that was not going to impress these officers.

"It's Mrs. Porter, right?" Grant asked.

"That's right. I'm Mrs. Clemons' sister and I have to say I'm upset that you're bothering her with questions again."

"I know it's difficult for everyone, but we want to find out who killed your brother-in-law just as much as you do. And that means a lot of questions."

Lina sat down firmly next to Rachel. "Well, I think you've pestered her enough for one day."

"Lina, please – it's OK."

"No, it isn't, Rachel. You need your rest. And you," with a sharp look at the two officers, "need to go. You can come back or call another time. Or ask me. But my sister's had enough for now."

"It's hard on everyone," Grant said. "Believe it or not, we don't like asking questions any more than you like answering them. But we have to if we're going to find out who killed your brother-in-law – and your husband," he added, looking again at Rachel.

Lina sat back slightly. "I know you have to do your jobs," she said, "But it's heartless and pointless to keep bothering Rachel."

"She's lucky to have someone close by who cares about her," Grant said. It didn't work. Lina continued to glare at him.

Then, he changed the subject. "Since you're here, Mrs. Porter, maybe you could answer a couple of questions?"

"I don't see how I can be of any help, but go ahead."

"Do you know of anyone who would have wanted to kill your brother-in-law?"

"No, not at all. He never mentioned anything, and I couldn't imagine anyone who'd want to hurt him."

Grant looked at Enders, then back at Lina. "Did you know about his other son – Victor Wagner?"
Lina thought for a moment. Then she looked at Rachel. "I did," she finally said. "But I don't think that has anything to do with anything. It was years ago. Ron and Rachel weren't even together at the time. You're just humiliating her by bringing it up. Now, unless you want to ask me something that actually has to do with Ron's death, I think you should leave."

The two officers looked at each other again. What were they saying to each other in that silent language? Whatever it was, it meant they were getting ready to leave. They both rose to their feet. But they weren't quite ready to give up yet. Grant turned to Rachel. "So, you're certain, Mrs. Clemons, that you haven't been out of town in the last week?"
"Absolutely certain. You can check anything you want. I haven't been anywhere except local places."
"There. You have your answer," Lina said belligerently.
"Thanks very much," the young officer said. Then the two left.

They'd seemed satisfied with her answers, Rachel thought. And no thanks to Lina. She went back into the house where she found Lina in the kitchen pouring herself a glass of juice. "Why did you have to do that?" she asked a little testily
"Do what?"
"Be so rude to those cops. They're just doing their jobs."

"They're harassing you. They think that just because you were Ron's wife, you're – you know something about what happened to him."

"You think they suspect me, don't you?" Rachel found it hard to keep the tremor out of her voice.

"No, of course not. I mean, they're suspicious of everyone, especially spouses. That's all. I don't think they suspect you any more than that. They're just covering themselves."

"Do you think they think I did it?"

"I don't see how they could. You and Ron loved each other."

Ron. Ron going to the refrigerator for a cold drink. Getting ready to cut the grass. Rachel shook her head a little. "Ron was a good person,' she said slowly. 'Look, I'm sorry, but I need some rest."

"Of course. You go on upstairs. I'll just finish this and be on my way."

Luke and Grant hadn't said much to each other on the way back to the station. But now, as they pulled into the parking lot, Luke said, "So, do you think she's telling the truth?"

"Who, the widow?"

"Yeah."

"I think she is. She's not stupid. She's got to know we're going to check on what she says and find out if she's gotten any rental cars or plane tickets or stayed in a hotel."

"But if it wasn't her…"

"…Who else would it be, right?"

"Exactly."

"I don't know."

Then an idea came to Luke. "I noticed something while we were there."

"What's that?" Grant paused after he took the key out of the car's ignition.

"Those two women are sisters, right?"

"Yeah."

"They look a lot alike, don't you think?"

Grant nodded slowly. "I've been thinking about that too. But the only problem is, we don't have a motive for the sister. Not an obvious one, anyway. And besides, people can put wigs on, different makeup, heels or whatever. Just the fact that the woman we're looking for has the same color hair and is about the same height as those women doesn't mean much."

"That's true. But the sister could have a motive, couldn't she?"

"She could. Follow up your idea. Visit her, maybe talk to her, but don't get blinded. You know what happens when you assume something, don't you?"

"Yeah, I do," Luke grinned as he and Grant went into the building.

Ten

Patricia looked up from her computer as Luke and Grant walked in. 'Glad you're here,' she said.
"You got something?" Luke asked.
"I don't know. Could be. I called Mid-Atlantic like you asked," she looked at Grant, who nodded. "Of the people we're interested in, only two have been out of town this week. One is Denise Bascomb and the other is Trent Rakins. Rakins went to a trade show in Boston. I'm waiting for confirmation on his hotel and rental car, but the airline confirmed his flight there and his return flight."
"Besides," Luke said. "We're looking for a woman, aren't we?"
"Yeah, but it's still good to know where everybody was," Grant said. He was right, Patricia thought. Then Grant looked back at her. "And Bascomb?"
"That's what's interesting. She went to a seminar – in Chicago."
"Chicago?"
Patricia nodded. "That's what I thought too. I got confirmation of her flight and hotel."
"She stayed in Chicago?"
"Yeah, right in town."

Grant sat down, leaning slightly towards Patricia and wearing his 'I'm listening intently' facial expression. "Did she rent a car?"
"She did. Turns out it was a dark blue Toyota Corolla."
"Yeah?"
"Exactly. Victor Wagner says that the woman who bought him the coffee had a dark blue Toyota."
"Lot of dark blue Toyotas out there though."

[188]

Patricia nodded and picked up her notebook. She flipped through it until she came to the page she wanted. "I know. And Wagner says the woman who gave him the poisoned coffee had reddish-brown hair. Denise Bascomb's a blonde. Not natural, but still. Of course, she could have worn a wig or something."

"We can't rule her out, anyway. What about Emma Yeats?"

"She's been in town. Confirmed by a few fellow employees. Besides, there's no sign of a motive. No indication that there was an affair or anything like that, and by all accounts, she got along well with Clemons. Anything's possible, but it just doesn't seem likely."

Now Luke spoke up. "What if we ask Wagner to take a look at pictures of these women? Of Rachel Clemons, of Denise Bascomb, of Emma Yeats, and of Lina Porter?"

Lina Porter? Patricia hadn't thought of that, damnit. But it was a possibility. She couldn't think of a motive, but Luke was right to include her. You could never tell. "I like that idea," she said.

"Me too," added Grant. "Enders, get some recent photos. Try to get really clear shots if you can. Then get them to Palatine and have Wagner see if he recognizes anyone."

Then Patricia had an idea. "We're going on the assumption that the woman who poisoned Victor Wagner is the same woman who met Clemons at the coffee place, right?"

"That's right," Grant said.

"Would it make sense if I showed those pictures there? See if somebody recognizes somebody?"

"Good idea," Grant said. He wasn't exactly lavish with his praise, so this meant something. "Enders, make sure you give Stanley clear copies of whatever pictures you get. I also want you to visit Lina Porter. Find out what she can tell you. And don't forget the foxglove. And I want to know where we are before you're done for the day."

"Got it."

"Will do."

Two hours later, Patricia walked into A Taste of Home, armed with the copies Luke had given her. She glanced at her watch; it was two-thirty, half an hour until the café closed. She and Luke had agreed to meet back at the police station at five, so they could make a few visits together, so she had plenty of time. Fortunately, Lucy Westmark was on duty. Patricia took a seat at the counter and waited until Lucy came over and mechanically asked, "What can I get you?"

"Cup of decaf, please."

Lucy nodded and then glanced up. Her face became a little more animated as she recognized Patricia. 'Hey, you're that" – she lowered her voice a little – "that cop that was here the other day, aren't you?"

"Yup, that was me."

"You need to talk to me again?'"

"If you have a minute."

"We're not busy. Just give me a sec."

Patricia nodded, and Lucy went off to deliver two other orders. Five minutes later she was back, this time with Patricia's order.

"What's this – what did you need to ask me?"

"Do you remember the other day when you told me you recognized this man?" Patricia showed Lucy the photograph.

"Yeah, like I said, nice guy."

"And then you said you saw him in here with a lady that last time. Is that right?"

"Yeah, that's right."

"Does any of these women look like her?" Patricia put the set of photographs on the counter facing Lucy, who asked, "Can I pick them up?"

"Yes, you can. Just please be careful with them."

"I will.'"

Patricia took a sip of her coffee as Lucy picked up the pictures one by one, looking closely at each. After a moment, she pointed to the picture of Emma Yeats. "It wasn't her," she said firmly. "I've seen her with that guy here before. I don't know her name but I'm pretty sure they worked together. That's how they acted, anyway."

"OK, what about the others?"

Lucy looked at them again. "That's harder. I don't think it was her though,' and she pointed towards the picture of Denise Bascomb. 'Wrong color hair and she's been in here before with that guy, too, I think." Then she wrinkled her brow. "Sorry. I don't think it was her, but I couldn't swear it wasn't. I mean, with makeup or whatever, it could be."

"That's OK. Just do the best you can. You're helping a lot."

Brightening up a bit, Lucy looked at the last two pictures. "These two have the right color hair. And they look about right too. It might be either of them."

Patricia drank more of her coffee and then removed the pictures of Denise and Emma. "Take a closer look at those two. If it was one of those two women, which one do you think it might be?"

Lucy laughed a little. "This is worse than a test in school." Then she looked at the remaining two pictures again. She picked each one up and put it down. Then she picked both up and looked at them side by side. "There's something about her," she finally said, handing the picture to Patricia.

"Something familiar?"

Lucy nodded. "Like I said, I can't be a hundred percent sure. I don't want to get anyone in trouble or anything." A sudden look of concern crossed her face as she thought about the implications of identifying someone who was seen with a murder victim.

"I understand. I'm not here to arrest anybody. We just want to follow up on all the leads we can get."

"Well in that case, if I had to choose, I'd say it was her." She'd chosen the photograph of Lina Porter. "But I could be wrong," she added hastily.

"That's fine. Let's just say you think she looks familiar."

"Yeah, that's about right.'"

"Thanks. That's a very big help."

Patricia gathered up the photographs and reached into her pocket for her wallet. Lucy put up a hand to stop her and said, "It's on the house. I want you to catch the bastard who killed that guy. I never really knew who he was, but I liked him."

"I appreciate it," Patricia pulled her hand out of her pocket. "And we will do the best we can to catch whoever did it."

She tucked the pictures into her pocket and left the café.

At the Palatine Police Station, Officer Caroline Drackmann was answering her email when the receptionist interrupted her. "Sorry, but someone's here to see you."

"What's the name?"

"Wagner. Victor Wagner."

"Right," Drackmann nodded. "I'll be there in a second."

"I'll tell him."

"Thanks."

A minute later, Drackmann got up from her desk and went to the large door that separated the waiting room from the rest of the station. She immediately recognized Wagner and walked over to him.

"Thanks for stopping by," she said as they shook hands.

"Not a problem. Anything I can do to help."

He followed her through the door and back to her desk, where she indicated a seat in front of it. After he'd sat down, she said, "I'm going to show you some pictures. I want you to look at each one and see if any of them looks like the woman you stopped to help."

"All right. I can't swear I'd recognize her again, but I'll sure try."

"You'll probably do better than you think you will. Here we go." She placed the pictures face down in front of him. "Now, I want you to look at each one. Take your time and don't worry. There are no right or wrong answers here."

Victor picked up the first picture. "Nope. Not her."

"You're sure."

"Absolutely. This woman is too young. Besides, it's hard to tell but I think she's too short." He pushed the picture of Emma Yeats back towards Drackmann and turned over the next picture. Drackmann waited silently while he studied it. He put it down and tapped it. "Hard to tell. I don't think the woman I met was a blonde. But she had a hat on. Besides, women can wear wigs or dye their hair or whatever, right?"

"They sure can. Try to look really carefully at her face and see if it rings a bell."

He did. "It's possible," he finally said slowly. "I don't *think* it was her, but it could be." And he slid the picture of Denise Bascomb across the desk. Drackmann took it and waited while he looked at the other two pictures. This time he studied both for a while. Then he shook his head. "It could easily have been one of these two women. They have the right color hair. But with the hat and all, it's so hard to say. It's just…the hair caught my attention."

"Fair enough. Now, just for a minute, pretend you've only seen these two pictures. Could you guess which one of them was the woman you met?" Victor looked from one to the other of the pictures a few times. Finally, he ran a hand through his hair and said, "It's so hard because they resemble each other. But maybe this one?" He pointed to the picture of Lina Porter.

"Are you sure?"

"No. That's the problem. I'm not. Not sure the way you'd have to be in court, I mean. It could have been either of those two women. Or that blonde if her hair was dyed or something. I only know it wasn't the brunette."

"That's fine. All we need is your best guess."

"Sorry I can't be of more help. I wish I'd paid more attention."

"It's OK. It's hard to remember anyway after a little time has passed."

"That's just it. And I've been sick."

"I know. I hope you're better now."

"I am, thanks. Over the hump, anyway."

"Good. We may need to speak to you again, so please let me know if you travel, OK?"

"I will. And thanks. I hope you'll get this person. I'm worried about my family."

"I can imagine. I would be too. And we are doing everything we can."

"I know you're doing your best. Please don't think I'm unaware or ungrateful. It's just that, well, it's my family. My baby hasn't even been born yet."

"It would be enough to scare anyone. We are working on it though. As soon as we know anything, I'll be in contact."

"All right. In the meantime, do you think we need to do anything? Go somewhere else?"

"Honestly," Drackmann put down the pen she was holding. "I don't believe there's any immediate danger to you or to your wife. I don't want you to be at risk any more than you want it, so I would tell you if I thought you should take some time away. For now, just be careful about answering the door or the telephone."

Victor nodded. "We're already doing that. And we're watching our emails too."

"That's good. And right now, that's all you can do." Victor let her words sink in for a minute. Then he nodded again and thanked her as he left.

Denise Bascomb pulled into the residents' parking lot of the building where she had her condominium.

[195]

She'd chosen the place as much for its setting as for anything else, and so far, she loved living there. The community was a bit of a drive from her office, but she didn't care; it was quiet and felt almost rural. The grounds were well-kept, but it didn't feel too manicured. There were plenty of oak and maple trees, and the landscapers kept the outdoor gardens beautiful. Now, as she got out of her car, Denise saw that the trees were already getting new leaves, and some of the plants in the garden were almost ready to flower. Still, it was only the end of March; it wasn't unknown for a cold snap to stop everything in its tracks.

Denise crossed the parking lot and went into her building, stopping first at the row of mail slots just beyond the front door. She inserted her mail key, opened the box and reached in. It was odd to feel nothing but the cold metal sides and bottom of the box. Usually there were at least some ads or bills. Oh, well, one less thing to worry about. She went up the short flight of stairs to the second floor of the building where she had her own condominium. She put her key into the look only to realize that the door was unlocked. She drew her hand back and caught her breath. Who the hell would be in her condo?

She took a few steps backwards and as quietly as possible, she pulled her phone out of her purse. She pushed the "Power" button and was just about to call the police when the door opened.
"Greg! What are you doing here?" she gasped.
"You scared the hell out of me!"

"Sorry," he said, shifting the bag he was carrying from one arm to the other. "Didn't you get my voice mail?"

"You sent me a voice mail?"

"Yeah, about an hour ago. I tried to call you, but you weren't picking up."

"I was in a client meeting. I always turn my phone off when I meet with clients. I just now turned it back on." She glanced down at the phone that was still in her hand. Sure enough, the green message indicator light was flashing. Sheepishly, she dropped the phone back into her purse. "Well, anyway, what are you doing here?" she asked when she'd recovered her composure.

"Let me take this trash out," Greg said, jerking his chin towards the bag in his hand. "Then we'll catch up."

"OK," Denise said, holding the door so he could use both hands to hold the bag. "And thanks."

She went inside and put her purse on a small circular glass table by the door. Then she sagged into the armchair next to the table. Greg had startled her more than she'd realized at first. She was pulling off her pumps when he came back in. He gestured towards the small pile of mail on the edge of the kitchen counter. "Thought I'd save you a stop, and I got your mail." Then he sat on the sofa facing the chair.

She looked up at him. "So what's going on?"

"I want to talk about your trip to Chicago."

"To Chicago? That was – what? – a week ago?"

"Exactly."

"So? What about it?"

"You went to the trade show, right?"

"That's right, but you already knew that. Why the questions?"

"You weren't back until two days after the trade show ended."

"And? I decided to stay a couple of extra days. I like Chicago. What's the big deal, anyway? It's not like I'm asking to be reimbursed for those extra days."

"I know that. That's not the point. I just – I just wondered what you were doing, that's all."

Then it hit her. "You're jealous, aren't you, Greg? Do you think I met someone there?"

Greg looked down at his shoes. Then he slowly looked up at her. "Did you?"

"Did I what? No! Of course I didn't meet anyone there."

Greg relaxed a little and said, "I'm sorry. I shouldn't care – I know I shouldn't. It's not up to me if you travel. But, well, we're together. I just – I don't know."

Denise got up and moved over to the sofa, where she looked down at Greg. "Look," she said, a little sharply. "I know you don't like it that I'm not ready to move in with you. Well, not now, anyway. And I'm a long way from wanting to get married or do anything permanent. It was a big thing for me just to give you a key. But it doesn't mean I don't care about you. And it doesn't mean I'm sleeping with someone else behind your back. If I ever think it's over between us, I'll flat-out tell you. OK? You just have to trust me. And you don't get to check up on me!"

Greg nodded. "I know, I know. I'm sorry if that was too creepy. And I don't want to smother you. I just can't help it, though. I guess I get possessive. You know I'd do anything for you."

"I know." She took his hand. "And I appreciate it. And I promise, I'm not cheating on you, OK? Really. I'm not."

"All right." Greg shook his head slightly. Then, in a firmer voice, he changed the subject. "I know you didn't get my message, but do you have plans tonight? I thought maybe a movie?"

"Yeah, that works. Let me just get changed." Denise got up, heading towards the bedroom that was at the end of a short corridor. "Be right back," she called.

Greg pulled his phone out of his pocket and sat back down. He'd just started to play a game on it when the doorbell sounded. He heard Denise's muffled shout, "Will you get that? It's probably some salesman or something."

"OK," he called back. He went to the door and looked through the peephole. Instead of a salesperson, he saw a police badge. He opened the door part of the way. There were the same two cops that he'd talked to before. The young woman – he couldn't remember her name – said, "Is Ms. Bascomb in?"

"Um, yes, she is. I guess you should come in." They both came in and he waved them to the sofa. "She's just getting changed," he explained. "She'll be out soon. What's this about?"

"We really need to speak to Ms. Bascomb," was all the officer said.

After a minute or two more, Denise came out of the bedroom, dressed in jeans, a royal blue corduroy shirt and matching low-heeled boots. She'd taken her hair out of its usual ponytail; now it fell over her shoulders like a curtain. "Who was it, Greg?" she called. Her voice trailed off as she saw the two police officers.

"Ms. Bascomb? You may remember us. I'm Officer Stanley and this is Officer Enders. We've spoken to you a couple of times."

"Yes, of course, I remember," Denise said, sitting slowly down in the armchair. "Is this about Ron Clemons' death again?"

"Partly. We're just checking up on a few things and we have a couple of questions for you."

"All right."

Officer Stanley looked around the living room. "How long have you lived here?"

"In this condo? A couple of years."

"It's nice. Do you have a yard area outside, too?"

"No. Just as well, too. I'm not much good with plants."

"I'm not, either."

The police officer looked down at her notes. "Your secretary said you were in Chicago for a few days recently. Is that right?"

"Yes, for an annual trade show."

"And you were there for how many days?"

"Three."

"Did you stay in the city the whole time?"

"Yes. Wait – why are you asking me these questions? Has something happened?"

"There's been an incident in the Chicago area that may be related to Mr. Clemons' death."

"What incident? What happened?"

The two officers looked at each other. "It was an attempted murder."

"And you think I had something to do with it?"

[200]

"We're just getting information right now, Ma'am. You left Chicago on the day the conference ended?"

"That's right."

"And you got back that night?"

"I think so."

"All right," Officer Stanley said, making a note in her notebook. "For now, that's all we need. We'll be in touch if we need any other information, so please don't travel without letting us know."

"No, I won't."

The officers thanked both Denise and Greg as they left. Then Greg turned to Denise. "You lied to them," he said, as though he didn't want to believe what he was saying.

"No, I didn't. I told them about being at the trade show."

"Yes, but you didn't come back when it ended. You came back two days later. We were just talking about it before they came."

"Look, it doesn't matter. I spent a little extra time in Chicago, that's all. I didn't leave the city, and that's what they seemed to care about."

"You should still tell them about it."

"We're not going to worry about it right now. If they call or come back or something, I'll explain. Don't have a fit, OK? And for God's sake don't say anything to them. Let me straighten it out if I have to."

"But you will, right?"

"Of course I will. Now let's go online and pick a movie to go see."

As they got into the police car, Patricia asked Luke "So what do you think?"

"You mean about Denise Bascomb?"

"Yeah. Do you think she's telling the truth?"

"She's in sales. A lot of salespeople are very good at making you believe exactly what they want you to believe. She could be telling the absolute truth. Or not. Hard to know if she's as good at her job as they say she is."

Patricia nodded. She was glad they were thinking along the same lines.

"So what now? We check on what she said?"

"I think so. We ought to make sure it tallies with the days she said. If it does, we leave it alone and concentrate on the widow and her sister. If not, we have another talk with our sales leader."

"OK. One thing, though. It doesn't seem like she has foxglove here."

"No, she probably doesn't. But you can buy it and use it and get rid of it."

"Yup."

Luke checked his watch. "Since we're out anyway, let's take a quick ride to Lina Porter's home. She ought to be home from work by now."

"OK." Patricia looked up the address and put it into the car's GPS system. "It's not too far," she said when the directions came up.

Twenty minutes later, they got to the Porters' home. "Nice place," Luke muttered as they got out of the car.

They looked around at the yard as they walked towards the door. The sun hadn't set yet, but it would be getting dark before very long.

"You see anything?"

Patricia shook her head. "No. Well, anyway, no foxglove." There were a few different kinds of flowers, some juniper shrubs, and a few other things, plus some bare patches, but not what they were looking for.

By the time they got to the front door, Lina had already seen them coming. "You're the police officers who were at my sister's house, aren't you? The ones who are trying to find out what happened to Ron?"

"That's right. We have a couple of questions for you."

"For me? I don't see how I can be of any help at all."

"Just a couple of things," Patricia insisted. "It won't take long."

"All right," Lina sighed. "You'd better come in." Once she'd seated them in the living room (no mention of coffee, tea, or anything else), Luke began. "You don't live very far from your sister. Do you see her often?"

"Every few days, but what does that have to do with anything?"

"Well, you'd notice if something seemed off, or if either Mrs. Clemons or her husband were ill."

"I would, but I didn't. They were both just fine. And before you ask, they weren't fighting or anything, either. Everything was normal."

"It must have been a real shock, then, to hear about Mr. Clemons' death." This came from Patricia.

"Well, it was," Lina turned to Patricia and nodded. Was that a slight thaw in her reaction? "To be honest, I don't think it's really hit home yet."

Luke and Patricia exchanged a glance. Patricia glanced down at the notebook she'd pulled out of her pocket. "So, Mr. and Mrs. Clemons had a solid relationship?"

"Absolutely. Why wouldn't they?" Nope. No thaw at all.

Patricia took a breath. "Did Mrs. Clemons say anything to you about Victor Wagner?"

"Victor who? Oh, him. No, she didn't. And even if she did, it wouldn't matter. She loved her husband and wouldn't have done anything to hurt him."

Take that!

Luke came to the rescue. "We have to ask all sorts of questions if we're going to get to the truth about what happened to Mr. Clemons."

"I'm sure you do, but that doesn't mean you can insult my sister! Now, if you're done, I'd like to get my dinner started."

No sense in making matters worse. Patricia and Luke thanked Lina for her time and left. When they were out of earshot, Patricia muttered, "Not the best interview we ever had."

"No, but she did at least confirm that the Clemons weren't fighting or anything."

"True. And did you notice? No Foxglove. I see lots of other plants and some shrubs and trees, but no foxglove."

"You think she'd come out with a pitchfork if we checked the back?"

"Probably, but we should at least peek."

They both glanced back at the door, which was now defiantly shut. Nobody looking out the windows, either. They walked around to the backyard gate and took a quick look. No foxglove. "We'd better get going," Luke suggested, "Or she really might come out here with a weapon."

Eleven

Two o'clock in the morning and Patricia was still
wide awake, watching the shadows from the trees
outside chase each other across the bedroom ceiling.
She was glad to hear Becky's deep, even breathing
beside her. It wasn't Becky's fault that Patricia
hadn't been able to fall asleep.

They always warned cops not to bring their jobs
home, but TV shows and crime novels were full of
fictional police who did. It made for drama and
probably for high ratings, but it wasn't the way
Patricia wanted to live her life. And so far, she'd
been fairly well able to keep work at work and
home at home. But this was a murder. Dr. Zara was
right. The fact that it was murder just brought
everything back. Serena. Her smile. The way the
sun sparkled on her dark hair the day they met.
Eating ice cream at Sweet Dreams. Serena's
parents, who would never be the same. And
Patricia's own ache.

It wasn't fair to Becky, thinking about that hurt. But
it was there. It made no sense to pretend that it
wasn't. It had twisted Patricia into a new shape. It
was hard to get used to this new self. Sometimes it
felt as though she was an entirely different person –
one she didn't always like very much at all. She
wondered what Becky would have thought of her if
they'd met before Serena died. As it was, poor
Becky had to deal with the shattered pieces. Well, it
wasn't as though Patricia hadn't been honest with
her. She'd told Becky right from the beginning

about Serena and what had happened. Becky had said she understood, and she really did try. She didn't get upset when Patricia talked about Serena's violin playing, or the way her laugh sounded. She even said it didn't bother her, and Patricia hoped it didn't. But there were just some pieces of Patricia that were out of her reach.

She rolled over on her side and watched the shadows dance on the wall opposite the window. This isn't any good at all. You're letting this poisoning case get to you, exactly the thing you were told *not* to do. If it were any other kind of case, or if it weren't a murder, it wouldn't get to you at all. But it did. She couldn't deny it. She rolled slightly in the other direction and peeked over her shoulder at Becky. Good, she was sleeping soundly. Enough obsessing about how this case made her feel. She needed to try to sleep.

It didn't work though. After a few more minutes, Patricia gave up trying to calm herself down. She slipped out from under the covers and padded as silently as she could to the closet. She picked up her navy-blue terrycloth bathrobe from its hook and wrapped herself in it. With another glance at Becky's sleeping form, she left the bedroom, silently closing the door behind her. No sense in waking Becky up just because she couldn't sleep.

She went into the kitchen, opened the pantry door and stood staring at it for a moment. Then she pulled out the box of chamomile tea. Becky always said it helped calm the nerves. She chose a packet and made herself a cup of tea. Then she took the tea into the living room and flicked on the television.

Not that there was much to watch at that hour. Home shopping, a 1950's Grade Z horror film, reruns of comedy shows she never watched in the first place, and not a lot else. And she didn't have the energy to search through Netflix. Finally, she settled on a documentary about dinosaurs and their fossils. She was staring at it, not really paying much attention when she heard a noise behind her.

"I thought I'd find you here," Becky said.

"Did I wake you? I'm sorry,"

"You didn't. I had to go to the bathroom."

Becky sat down on the sofa beside Patricia.

"Watcha watching?"

"Some documentary. To be honest, I'm not paying a lot of attention to it."

"What's wrong?"

"Nothing – I mean, nothing huge and major. I just can't sleep."

"What's on your mind? You always get like this when you're worried about something."

"Just – I don't know. I guess it's this poisoning case. It's…"

"…waking up all the monsters, isn't it?"

Patricia turned a miserable face towards her. "I'm sorry, Beck, I can't help it."

"Why do you need to help it?"

"Because none of this is your fault. I just let this get to me, I guess, and it's bringing up a lot of things."

"We can talk about it if you want."

"It's not going to help anything."

Becky drew back slightly. "Neither is keeping everything stuffed inside. Sometimes I feel like I can't even reach you."

Patricia tried to explain. "I'm still here, you know. It's just hard sometimes."

"Well, it's hard for me, too."

"What are you talking about?"

"When you won't even tell me what's on your mind, you shut me out. I hate that!"

"I'm not shutting you out," Patricia's tone sharpened a little. "I just don't want to hurt you."

"But that's just it! You're hurting me more when you *won't* talk to me."

"I'm not trying to hurt you. I'm just trying…"

"To what? Protect me?"

"Maybe."

"I don't need protection. I'm all grown up." Becky's voice was low and hard, her angry tone.

"I know you are, but –"

"– And when you won't confide in me, it's like you don't trust me. Is that it? You don't trust me?"

"Of course I do!"

"Then don't keep running away like that!"

"I'm not running away. I'm right here."

"You know what I mean. You're here but you're not here."

"I am trying, Beck."

"I know," Becky's voice softened, but only a little. 'But you have to stop trying to protect me. I'm not that fragile. And I don't like being shut out."

"I'm not shutting you out on purpose."

"Well, that's what it feels like." Becky ran a hand through her hair. "Look, it's way too late for this. I'm going back to bed."

She got up and left the living room. Patricia watched her leave, then flopped back against the sofa cushion. What the hell had *that* been about? She almost didn't want to know. All she was trying to do was not to take her own pain out on Becky. Still, Becky was right about being grown up. Why is it that the one thing you do to be kind to someone ends up being taken as an insult?

Four hours later, Luke Enders pulled up to the police station. He'd gotten an early start, which meant he might even have beat his partner in. He looked out the windshield through the misty drizzle that distorted his view. No Patricia. With a self-satisfied smile that he couldn't quite help, he got out of his car and went inside, ducking his head just a bit as the drizzle tried to turn into rain.

He'd just settled in at his desk and turned on his computer when Patricia came in. He was just about to tease her about being lazy when he took a closer look at her. The dark circles under her eyes and barely-combed hair spoke volumes.
"You're looking fabulous this morning," he said in what he hoped was a light tone.
"Screw you!" Patricia snapped. Then she stopped herself and looked at Luke apologetically. "Sorry. I didn't mean that. It's just..."
"You don't need to explain. You OK?"
"I will be." She glanced around. "Becky and I had an argument, that's all. No big deal."
Luke didn't normally like to get involved in anyone's personal life. It was just easier that way. But he did care about his partner. "Nothing serious, I hope."
"Nothing that can't be fixed.'"

At least Patricia hoped so. She and Becky didn't usually argue, so when they did, it was hard on both of them. She was going to have to deal with that later though. Right now, she had to get her mind on the job before Grant got in. She sat down at her desk, turned on her computer and looked across at Luke, who was flipping through some incident reports.

"We need to put that stuff online," she said. Might as well hold out the olive branch.

Luke took it. "Yeah, this stuff isn't even searchable," he answered, gesturing at the papers in front of him. "Makes no sense at all."

"No, it doesn't. Anything I need to know about before we dig in?"

"Don't think so."

Patricia nodded and got to work on her email in-box.

When she'd finished with her email, Patricia followed up on Denise Bascomb's car rental history. She started with a call to the woman herself, although it was still early (No, I don't mind. I was getting ready for work anyway). After asking about any car rental records (I think so. It'll probably be on my last expense report.), Patricia asked Denise to send her a copy of the rental paperwork as soon as possible (Sure. Soon as I get to the office.). That would mean about half an hour wait on the car rental information.

While she waited, Patricia turned her attention to Greg Isaacson's background. They were looking for a woman, but Grant was right about checking everyone. You never knew. And it was obvious that Isaacson had it bad for Denise Bascomb. She accessed the department's database and ran Isaacson's name through it. After a few minutes, she had her answer. The guy had a fairly clean record. One speeding ticket a year ago (paid in full). No other prior arrests, no orders of protection, and no outstanding warrants. In short, nothing to raise eyebrows. Just to cover all possibilities, she'd try to find out whether he'd been in town when Victor Wagner was poisoned. But for now, it didn't seem likely he himself was involved.

About twenty minutes later, the receptionist on duty brought Patricia a sheet of paper. "I think this is for you," she said as she handed it over.

"Thanks," Patricia smiled and took the paper. Just as she'd hoped, it was a copy of Denise Bascomb's rental agreement.

"What's that?" Luke asked.

"It's Denise Bascomb's car rental agreement. Looks like she wasn't anywhere near Palatine when Victor Wagner was poisoned."

Luke stretched out his hand for the paper. When Patricia gave it to him, he looked at it a little more closely. "Wait a minute."

"What?"

"This isn't the final sign-off sheet. This is just the agreement. It only has estimated dates, times and costs."

Patricia took the paper back. "*Shit*! You're right! Now I'm going to have get hold of the car rental company."

It was all going to take time, Lina thought as she took a sip of tea. After a few days' break (after all, as she'd told her bosses, someone had to help Rachel with Ron's funeral), she was back at work at the Tredyffrin Township Parks and Recreation. She still didn't feel 'off duty' when it came to her sister, though. Rachel would need help for a long, long time. Maybe permanently. Well, that's what big sisters were for, after all. If only Rachel weren't so snappish about it. But then, Rachel had always been like that. Never listening to the people who cared about her. But at the same time, never much good at dealing with life without them.

"I guess I can't blame her too much," Lina said to herself as she looked at the list of spring events waiting to be scheduled. As if Ron's death hadn't been hard enough, there were the police. They just wouldn't leave Rachel alone. Lina had known the police would probably be asking questions, but this was ridiculous! The first thing she was going to have to do was get Rachel away somewhere for a long break. Yes, that was exactly what she'd do. Rachel might not be good at taking care of herself, but Lina knew what to do. With a satisfied nod, she went back to reviewing the activities that Parks and Rec. had approved for the late spring and summer. After that, she would put them all in the master schedule.

Rachel couldn't help herself. It was a relief to have Lina back at work. For some reason she couldn't have named, she craved solitude, and as helpful as Lina had been, there was no such thing as 'alone time' with her around. To Lina, any 'alone time' was The Enemy, to be avoided at all costs. But Rachel needed time right now. She would have to make plans. Thank God (and Ron!) she wouldn't have to worry about keeping the house or paying the bills. But it was more than that. There were dozens of decisions – hundreds – that had to be made.

Now Rachel sat silently at the kitchen table, looking out the window as the morning's drizzle started to get more insistent. Her window. Her kitchen. Her cups and plates and cutlery. She'd heard of people who lost their spouses, who couldn't stand living in the same house and felt the need to move. Leaving wouldn't be that easy for Rachel. There were too many pieces of herself right here. Of course, if she moved, she could be closer to Jason (no, don't think about Ron's other son – about Victor). That could be good for both of them. But no, Jason was a man now; he didn't want his mommy holding his hand and breathing down his neck. Besides, it really wouldn't be a good idea to leave just now.

Her mind made up for the moment, Rachel stood up, picked up the plate in front of her (what had she just eaten, anyway? She'd forgotten already) and put it in the dishwasher. Her telephone trilled just as she did. She looked at the display and made a face.
"Hi, Lina."
"What are you doing?"
"Just finished eating."
"Oh, that's great! You're eating!'"
"Yes, I'm eating, Lina." Why did Lina always have to sound exactly like a Kindergarten teacher when she talked?
"Well, good. Anyway," Lina's tone became a little less condescending, "why don't you come over for dinner tonight? I found a new lasagna recipe I want to try."
"Nah, I don't –"
"Ah, come on! You haven't been over in, well, in forever."

"All right, all right." Rachel was suddenly much too tired to argue.

"Great! Seven?"

"OK."

Success! Lina thought as she put her telephone back in her purse. Once she had Rachel relaxed and eating lasagna, it wouldn't take any effort at all to convince her she needed to get away. Now, there was only the matter of finding a good recipe...

"Well, that was interesting," Patricia said as she hung up her office telephone.

Luke put down the pile of witness statements he'd been shuffling through and looked up. When Patricia saw that she had his attention, she went on. "I just got off the phone with Regal Car Rental. It seems Denise Bascomb actually turned in her rental at Chicago O'Hare two days after she told us she did. They're emailing the invoice."

"That *is* interesting.' Luke raised his eyebrows. 'You think there's something in it?"

"I don't know for sure. I mean, for one thing," Patricia held up her right thumb, "I don't see a motive. For another,' now her right index finger, "there are other explanations. And we didn't find any foxglove where she lives."

"What do you mean no motive?"

"She had a motive for killing Ronald Clemons, but she didn't know that Victor Wagner was Clemons' son. Why the hell would she kill a random guy? And even if she somehow *did* know about Wagner, why would she kill him? Clemons was the immediate threat to her. Wagner had nothing to do with the company."

Luke nodded and leaned back in his chair. "So the only way she does this that makes any sense is if she has some connection to Wagner that we don't know about."

Now it was Patricia's turn to nod. "I guess so, but it just doesn't seem likely. I'd still like to know what she was doing during those two lost days."

"Probably for mature audiences only," Luke said.

"That leaves you out, then." A second later Patricia had to duck to avoid the wadded-paper missile that came flying at her head.

"Got a minute?" Greg Isaacson asked. He was standing in the open doorway to Denise Bascomb's office.

She looked up. There was that smile that made all kinds of promises. It never failed to draw him in. "Sure, what's up, Greg?"

He walked in, shutting the door behind him. Denise half-rose from her chair, and then sat back down when she saw his face. "What's wrong?" She gestured towards the caramel-colored leather chair opposite her own. Greg sat down and looked at her for a moment before saying anything.

"I need to ask you something," he finally said. She was going to hate this. She hated being questioned. "What?" Still a trace of that smile.

"What were you doing in Chicago?"

She sat straighter and put her forearms on the arms of her chair. "You know I was at the trade show. Why would you ask that?"

"Because I know you stayed for a couple of days after the trade show ended. You even told the police that. I want to know what you were doing."

Her eyes narrowed a little and got colder. "Do you still wonder if I was cheating on you or something?"

"I don't know what to think, Denise. I keep going over it and over it in my mind."

She shook her head just a bit. "I don't think I owe you an explanation, Greg. We talked about this. I don't have to report back to you about where I go and what I do."

He was going to have to back off a little. 'Look,' he said, lifting up his palms. "I'm not asking you for a minute-by-minute account of what you do. And I'm not trying to control you. It's just..."

"It's just that you don't trust me, isn't it?" Now her tone had gotten sharp.

"No, it's not that, either."

"Then what, exactly, is it?"

"What happens between us is between us. And you're right. You don't need to report back to me about what you do. But you lied to the police. That's serious."

"Is *that* what this is about? Damnit, Greg, I told you I'd deal with it. '

"But have you? You haven't even told me what's going on."

"OK, fine!" Then Denise looked away and back at Greg again. "I just needed some time to myself. Just for me. I'm being run ragged, and I wanted a break. That's all."

"You have been pushing yourself lately."

"That's what I mean. I just wanted to soak in a hot tub, go to a good day spa, the whole thing."

Then it hit Greg. "Why didn't you just tell the police that? There's nothing wrong with wanting some time to yourself."

[216]

"It doesn't give me a real alibi. I don't have any proof that all I did was pamper myself for two days. What do you think they'd do?"

"But you could have told me."

"I probably should have. It's just – it didn't seem important after Ron died. No big deal. No sense wasting time about it. In fact, let's just drop it, OK?" She moved back slightly in her seat and looked steadily at him, almost daring him to say anything more about it.

He took a step back. "All right. Dinner tonight?"

She nodded and gestured behind her at her desk. "OK, but I have to get back to it now."

He couldn't resist. He walked behind the desk and touched her hair, just barely. "Me, too. I'll see you later."

She nodded, and he left the office.

Greg had only gone a few feet down the hall when he saw two people coming towards him from the other direction. What the hell? What were those two cops doing here? Did they want to talk to him? No, if they did, they'd wouldn't have come up here, they'd have gone directly to his office. Denise? Maybe. Probably. Then they saw him, and Officer Stanley acknowledged him.

"Hello, Mr. Isaacson."

"Can I help you?" he asked as they moved closer.

"No, thanks. Not at the moment," Officer Enders said

"Ah, then you must be here to see Ms. Bascomb?"

"That's right. Do you know if she's in?"

"I think so."

"Thanks."

The two officers walked past Greg and towards Denise's office. Greg turned and watched them knock at her door. Had they found out she lied about her trip to Chicago? Probably. It had been really stupid of her to lie about that. They could check these things out. He hoped Denise would be OK. They'd probably rake her over the coals for not simply telling them she was looking at an acquisition. He'd just hang around for a bit – make sure she was all right. With a small nod to himself, he walked back towards her office and stopped just outside the door, which was open just a crack.

"...sorry, Officers. I know. I should have told you when you asked," Denise was saying.

"Why didn't you?"

"It wasn't a big deal. Nothing came of it. And I didn't want to go through the whole thing just then, that's all."

Then their voices dropped. Greg stepped closer to the door, but couldn't hear much:

"...Met some people...out for drinks...so it wasn't scheduled...that's right...But aren't most interviews...Usually, but..."

Interview? What was this about an interview? Maybe he'd heard wrong. Denise hadn't said a thing about an interview, and she definitely would have. Wouldn't she? The cold prickle wouldn't go away. What if she did have an interview? What if she'd decided to leave him and move to Chicago? Maybe she was just waiting for the right moment to tell him. The cold knot in his stomach got tighter as he thought about it. No, this is ridiculous. You're being too possessive. Just let it go. Nothing is wrong. Deep breath. Ask her later. Yes, that was it.

He would ask her later – at dinner. He had work to do now, and he wouldn't be able to get to it if he kept obsessing about something that was probably no big deal, anyway. Drawing a long breath to steady himself, Greg turned around and went back towards his office.

"So what do you think?" Patricia asked Luke as they got back into their police unit.
"I don't know," Luke shook his head slowly, buckled his safety belt and looked in the mirrors. "She wasn't exactly honest with us the first time we talked to her. That tells me she doesn't have a problem lying to us."
"Sure seems that way. But that doesn't mean she's the one," Patricia continued as Luke steered the cruiser into traffic. "Like we said before, it could be a lot of things."
"True. I can't wait to hear what that Chicago company says about it all."
Patricia nodded. She wondered what the company would say, too.

She didn't have long to wait. When they got back to the station, Luke said he had some follow-up telephone calls to make. He'd started to look into what Rachel Clemons and Lina Porter had been doing when Victor Wagner was attacked. Now he wanted to talk to the Palatine Police again and see if they had any new information. While he did that, Patricia would call to check up on what Denise Bascomb had told them.

As Luke got settled in his desk chair, Patricia went to the ladies' room and then got a bottle of water from the vending machine in the break room. Why did it have to cost so much just to get some water? She wouldn't normally waste her money on bottled water, but the tap water in the ladies' room tasted too metallic. She'd heard they were going to get a water delivery service, but she hadn't seen any sign of it yet. Becky always said that bottled water was – Becky! What the hell was she going to do about Becky? There wasn't much she could do to patch things up right now. Hopefully she'd get out of here at a decent hour. Then maybe she could take Becky out somewhere nice for dinner. Something like that.

Now, Patricia went back to her desk and got the telephone number for Peerless Productions. Fortunately, it didn't take her long to get through to them. We're sorry, information on job applicants and interviews is confidential. Oh, the police? I'm sorry, but we can't give that information over the telephone. Email? Possibly, but only with authorization. That would be Mr. Michaelson – Kevin Michaelson, that's right. No, I'm sorry, he's not in. Tomorrow morning. Of course, I'll tell him you'd like to speak to him.
"It figures!" she muttered to herself as she hung up the telephone.

At five-thirty, Rachel locked her front door and slowly walked towards her car. She really couldn't come up with a good excuse not to go to Lina and Kyle's for dinner; and even if she could, Lina would fire back with so many alternate nights that it wouldn't be possible to get out of going. Might as well get it over with. Besides, the minute she seemed to have trouble coping, Lina would have her in a damned shrink's office. No, it would be better to go.

All too soon, she arrived at Lina and Kyle's ranch-style house and pulled into their driveway. Lina must have seen the car pull up; there she was in the doorway. No time for Rachel to sit and get herself together before getting out of the car. Here goes. She parked and stepped out, taking her time. Then she headed up the flagstone path to the door. By the time she got there, Lina had already come out onto the porch.

"You made it!" she exclaimed, hugging Rachel a little too hard. Rachel carefully detached herself and said, "Hi."

"Come on in! Kyle's just picking out a bottle of wine to open." She opened the door wider and Rachel walked past her into the foyer.

Ten minutes later, a glass of cabernet sauvignon in hand (Thanks, Kyle, it looks delicious!), Rachel was seated in the living room on the navy-blue sectional sofa. She was doing her best to follow what Lina was saying. Something about a cruise.

"…and so I said to Kyle, why don't we go on one of those Mediterranean cruises? They're supposed to be great."

"That's what I heard, too," Rachel answered. Stay focused. Don't zone out.

"And they don't cost as much as you'd think. They're actually pretty reasonable."

"So, did you decide to go ahead and book?"

"Not yet," Kyle said. "Not until after tax season, anyway. We'll probably book next month."

Spoken like a true accountant, Rachel thought.

Lina reached over and picked up a piece of basil-and-tomato bruschetta from the plate on the coffee table. "You know," she said, "You ought to think about getting away, Rachel."

"Me?"

"Of course. It's been so awful for you – with Ron and everything. Wouldn't it be great to just take some time away?"

Rachel shook her head. "I don't think so," she said, reaching for a slice of crusty garlic bread. She dipped it in the olive oil next to the loaf and shook her head again as she took a bite. Fresh, and chewy. Lina must have baked this herself.

"Why not?" Lina asked, eyebrows raised. Kyle's eyes crinkled with good humor as he sipped his wine. He knew what his wife could be like.

"I don't feel the need to get away," Rachel said. "There's a lot of work to do with the business. And where would I go, anyway?"

"I don't know. Maybe Boston. Spend some time with Jason."

"And do what? He's busy with his job and his wedding plans. He doesn't need his mother meddling. I already thought about that, and it just wouldn't make sense."

"Well, you ought to go somewhere. Take a break. Get away for a bit." Lina nodded emphatically.

Rachel listened patiently as Lina went on about the places she ought to go. You have time now, Rachel. You're still young. Travel. See the Grand Canyon. Go crazy in Vegas. Maybe even take a riverboat trip down the Mississippi. Something. Lina's words flowed out and gradually coalesced into an idea. After all, maybe it did make sense to get away. You heard about people doing that all the time after they

[222]

lost a spouse. Nobody would get upset about it. Everyone would probably be really supportive of it, actually, and that would be good.

"...don't want to get in too much of a rut, you know," Lina was saying.

Rachel tuned in again. "No, you're right about that."

"Exactly!"

"Maybe I'll go down to Ventnor or something. Watch some seagulls."

"You can go to Jersey any time you want. I'm talking something really different."

"Well...I always did think about taking a trip to wine country."

"There you go!" Lina smacked the cushion next to her for emphasis. "Napa would be great! They've got amazing food, great winery tours, the whole thing."

"Maybe I'll make some calls."

"No 'maybe' about it. You need to do this."

Or she will, Rachel thought. Time to change the subject before Lina got too excited. "OK, let me do some surfing and see what I find."

They heard a soft *ding* coming from the kitchen. "I think the lasagna's ready," Lina said. Thank God! Saved by the bell.

So far, dinner with Greg hadn't gone well, Denise thought. It probably would have been better if they hadn't seen each other tonight, but she didn't want to get up and leave the table now. He'd stopped by at seven, picked her up, and driven her to the restaurant with barely a sentence between them. The only conversation they'd had since getting here was to decide on the wine they wanted. She asked him what was wrong, but he just shook his head. Whatever it was, she hoped he'd just come out with it.

"So what is it?" she finally asked.

Greg lifted his water tumbler just a little and watched the ice swirling around in it. Then he put it back down and looked up. There was a look in his eyes that she hadn't seen before. It was almost as though he wasn't even there. "We need to talk," he finally said.

"This is it? 'The talk?'" she asked.

Even Greg smiled a little at that one. "Yeah, that did sound pretty stupid, didn't it?' Then his tone got serious. 'I need to talk to you about what happened today."

"What do you mean?'"

"I mean the cops coming to your office."

"You saw them?'"

"I was going down the hall. They were coming the other way."

"OK. So what? You know they've been asking questions about Ron's death."

"I know. That's not what I mean."

"Then what *do* you mean?"

He shifted a little in his chair and looked away for moment. "You're going to hate me for this."

"I could never hate you, Greg. Just tell me."

"I heard what you said to them. Something about an interview."

Shit! He'd heard. She'd have to do something. "You listened at the door, didn't you?"

Just then the sommelier came with their wine. They didn't look at each other as the bottle was opened and the wine started to flow. As soon as they were alone again, Denise returned to the attack. "You were listening! I can't believe you'd check up on me like that!"

"I wasn't – I didn't do it on purpose. I saw the cops, and I wanted to, well, be there for you in case you needed me for anything. I know, it sounds ridiculous. But I wasn't checking up on you."

"OK, so you heard me say something about an interview. What's the big deal?"

"The big deal? You interviewed for a job in Chicago and you didn't even tell me! Were you going to take the job and not tell me that, either? Why didn't you just tell me the truth in the first place?"

She put her hand on his, and he pulled it away.

"Look," she said. "I'm sorry I didn't say anything. Nothing came of it though. It didn't work out. It wasn't the job for me, and I'm not what they wanted, either. That's all."

"But you lied to me, and you didn't even let me know you had an interview!"

"It was one of those 'all of a sudden' things. I was at the show, met some people, we had some drinks, and they invited me to talk to them about a position. Simple as that. We talked. It wasn't going to happen. Thank you very much, nice to meet you. That's all it was."

"But you didn't even tell me that much. And we've seen each other every day since you've gotten back."

"It just didn't matter, Greg. It wasn't a big thing. It was like calling you to tell you I – I don't know – combed my hair or downloaded new software or whatever."

He took a sip of wine. "It's not just that, though."

She matched his sip. "What is it, then?"

"It's the whole thing. You lying to me and not telling me things. You lying to the police. I just don't know what to believe any more."

"Are you saying you don't trust me?"

"I'm saying sometimes you keep things from me. Things there's no reason for you to hide. I'd have understood if you wanted a new job. What the hell? We all want to do better. We could have talked about moving to Chicago or whatever. But you didn't say anything. What am I supposed to think?"

This was going to be harder than she'd thought.

"I'm sorry I didn't tell you. I didn't mean to hurt you. Don't hate me, OK?"

Now it was his turn. "I don't hate you. Never did. Just...stop keeping things from me. It makes me wonder what else I don't know."

"There's nothing else. I promise." Level gaze. Head slightly tilted to the right. Hand stretched out.

Greg finally took her hand and nodded slightly. It would be all right. Denise let out a silent, slow breath. She hadn't even realized she'd been holding it in.

"Excuse me. Are you folks ready to order?"

Denise had never been happier to be interrupted.

Should she stop at a florist and get some roses or something? No, Patricia thought. Becky's not much of a one for the grand gesture. Besides, she hates it when she thinks I'm wasting money. Especially for something we don't need. Something silly then? No, that'll just make her think I don't take her seriously. Patricia frowned as she sat through yet another cycle of lights. The traffic at this time of day could be awful. Finally, the light changed to green, and the line of cars slowly snaked forward.

[226]

This wasn't going to be a quick trip. At least the drizzle had let up.

After a few minutes, Patricia punched the Power button on the radio. She could use a distraction. After three tries (stupid advertisements!), she found a rock station. Just in time for the opening notes of Billy Joel's *Tell Her About It*. Patricia sang along, letting her mind drift a bit. Then it hit her. Of course! Trust Billy for the right idea. Becky wanted them to talk. Just talk. It must be hard to be a cop's partner. You had to keep so much in, even on the good days. There was a lot you couldn't talk about – a lot even the most loving partner wouldn't understand. It wasn't intentional, but it happened. It was easier to shut everything off than deal with it. No wonder Becky felt left out and lonely sometimes. OK, dinner and chatting it would be.

That plan got Patricia the rest of the way home. She went up the stairs, stopping to get the mail on the way (nothing important – just junk) and turned her key in the lock.
"Beck, you home?" she called out as she went inside.
A muffled sound from the bathroom told her where Becky was. Patricia dropped the mail on the coffee table in the living room and went through it to the kitchen. She was opening the refrigerator to get something to drink when she heard a sound behind her.
"Hey."
"Hi," she said. Becky took a step into the kitchen.
"Beck, I –'"
"Don't," Becky said, lifting a hand, palm out. "It's my fault. I get way too petty."

"But you're right. I hold a lot in. I have to. I'm working on it, though. I promise. Look, let's not wallow, OK? How about we go out somewhere, get some dinner. Then come back and do some Netflix."

"All right," Becky said. Then she looked down at herself. "I'm gonna have to shower and change. So will you. You look…"

"I know. Like shit. I'll shower and change, too."

"Baxter's or TJ's?"

"You pick."

"Baxter's."

Becky was so predictable sometimes. It was one of the things Patricia liked about her, actually.

"That's the thing, Beck," Patricia said, taking a sip of her Leffe Blond. They'd ordered their meals and were waiting for the food to arrive. "I'm pretty sure that sales rep didn't tell us the truth about what she was doing in Chicago, but Luke and I can't prove anything."

"So, you think she might have done it?" Becky asked. She took a pull of her Guinness Stout.

"I don't know. I mean, she has no motive to kill this guy. But she was in the area. Could be something totally innocent, but still. She lied. And she did have a motive to kill Ron Clemons."

"Maybe she's cheating on her boyfriend – the accountant guy."

"Could be. And maybe it's nothing. It's just that people who lie make me wonder about them."

Just then, the server brought their food, and for a few minutes, there was very little conversation as the two started to eat. Finally, Becky said, "What

[228]

about the wife? I mean the widow. You know what
I mean."

"Yeah, I know. It's possible. And there's no proof
she *didn't* go to Chicago. We're working on that
now, as a matter of fact. I just – I don't know. I
hope she's not the one."

"Why?"

"Something about her, I guess."

Becky nodded. She could guess, too. But she'd ask
about it later. The fragile peace was holding, and
she was in no mood to risk breaking it.

They finished their meal, mostly talking about
Becky's work. After dinner, they went home and, as
promised, Patricia opened up their Netflix account
on the TV. "Want to find a movie, or watch a TV
show?"

"Um…movie."

After a little more discussion, they settled on a
Humphrey Bogart film and brought blankets, extra
pillows, and a bowl of popcorn to the sofa. Then
they turned on the movie. About halfway through it,
Becky finally broached the subject.

"You know, Patricia, it's OK with me that you still
miss her."

Patricia squeezed Becky's hand. "You're amazing."

"No, I mean it. You're not supposed to just get over
something like that. She was murdered. You're
allowed to hurt about it."

Patricia snuggled closer. "I know. I couldn't help it
anyway. Sometimes it stabs me. Especially with this
poison case."

"I just – I want you to know you can talk to me
when it's that bad. I'm not jealous or anything. I'd
rather you talked to me, really."

"What do you mean?"

"I don't want you to shut me out. I hate that."
"I'll try. That's the best I can do right now. I'm sorry."
Becky nodded and put her head on Patricia's shoulder. "Just…don't freeze me out, OK? That's all I ask."
"I'm working on it." A tear formed at the corner of one of her eyes as Bogart did his thing.

Twelve

Napa travel packages weren't as expensive as Rachel had thought they were going to be. And they did look attractive. Maybe Lina had had a point last night. All of the Internet searches showed beautiful winery properties, comfortable tours and of course, luscious-looking food. And the weather! It looked as though it never rained at all in that part of California. Yes, she could definitely see spending some time there.

Rachel felt lucky that neither she nor Ron were what you'd call famous. At least she didn't have to cope too much with the media – just a couple of phone calls in the days right after Ron died. Nobody would even really notice if she were gone for a while. The more she thought about it, the more sense it made to just get away. Nodding to herself, she started planning where she might stay.

About ten minutes later, it hit her. Stupid that it had even taken that long. She wasn't going to be able to drop out of sight. Not really. Lina would have to know. Rachel couldn't even imagine the reaction Lina would have if she couldn't reach her, even for a day. Lina'd have the FBI and the National Guard troops for every state out searching. Probably the CIA and Interpol, too. And there were the police. They'd told her to let them know if she was planning to travel anywhere. They'd have to be able to reach her.

Rachel pushed her rolling chair a little away from her desk and tugged on her hair as she thought about the whole thing. There'd be no way to get around it: she was going to have to bring her cell phone with her. Her electronic leash. That was one thing she hadn't wanted to do, but it was going to be unavoidable. She sighed and turned her attention back to the screen. Gorgeous full shots of winery properties, the famous Napa Valley Wine Train, cozy-but-elegant B&Bs. If you wanted to take off for a while, Napa was at least a beautiful choice. And it was on the other side of the continent.

Luke Enders hung up his office telephone and glanced across to Patricia's desk. She looked up when she felt him watching her.

"Just got off the phone with the Palatine people," he told her.

"Yeah?"

He nodded and went on. "It seems Victor Wagner came in and tried to identify our Mystery Lady."

"Did they come up with anything?"

"Nothing definite. The only thing they said was that he told them it definitely wasn't" –Luke looked down at his hastily-scribbled notes – "Emma Yeats."

"Well, we didn't think she was the one, anyway, did we?"

"No, but still. It's nice to at least cross one person off the list."

Patricia thought about the name for a moment and got out her own notes. "And the waitress at the restaurant – the one where our guy had coffee the morning he died – said it wasn't Emma Yeats, either. She was pretty sure about it. Seems she's been there a couple of times, and the waitress recognized her from the picture I showed her."

[232]

"So now we have Denise Bascomb, Lina Porter and the wife, Rachel Clemons. They're the only ones who fit the description of the woman who went after Victor Wagner."

"And the waitress couldn't eliminate any of them."

"So, we check with Grant and then talk to them again."

Patricia nodded. She was still nervous about interviewing, but it was better than being stuck behind the desk all day. And maybe Grant wouldn't feel the need to babysit her any more if it went well. "Let me just make a few calls," she told Luke, "and I'll be right with you."

Denise had wakened that morning with a terrible headache, and it wasn't from the wine. It was just as well Greg hadn't stayed over last night. At least she'd had time to take some painkillers, sip her tea slowly and get her day started without angst. Now she sat at her desk trying to go over her copy of a contract she'd just signed with Marshall Higgins Jewelers. They were absolutely top of the market – just the kind of client she was good at getting and keeping. She should have been celebrating. Instead she could barely make sense of the words in front of her. Damn Greg and his insecurity! She rubbed her forehead and tried to focus again. *Tap tap* – the knock at her door made her look up. She glanced at her calendar application. No, she didn't have anyone scheduled.

"Come in," she said. A second later she regretted saying it.

"Good morning, Ms. Bascomb." Officer Stanley said. She was with the other young detective, Enders.

"Hello, Detectives. How can I help you?" As though she didn't know why they were there. Well, at least she could try to keep the visit short. She didn't offer them seats or coffee.

"We have a few things we need to clear up," said Enders.

"Will this take long? I have a meeting…'"

"Only a few minutes. Yesterday you told us you had a job interview while you were in Chicago, is that right?"

"Yes, that's right."

"You said the company's called Peerless, right?"

"Yes, Peerless Productions."

"We called them this morning. They have no record that you interviewed with them. In fact, they said they currently have no positions open in their Sales Department."

Denise looked pointedly at the time displayed on her computer. She drew in a breath and, with the same voice you hear from bored customer service representatives, she said, "It was a very informal interview. I didn't answer any advertisements or anything. I told you that."

"Yes, you did," said Officer Stanley. "But it's really unusual to have an interview and not have anyone remember you. If you could give us a few names of people you spoke to while you were there, we can clear the whole thing up."

"You don't expect me to have anything like that *here*, do you? I mean, it was a job interview. Not even an official interview. It was a casual 'what if' sort of a thing. I got a few business cards, that's all.

And I don't keep that kind of contact information in the office. I'll have to get it to you later." Score one for Denise.

"That'd be helpful. I can stop by your home later and get those contacts then."

So, Officer Stanley wasn't completely out of the game. "No, that won't be necessary," Denise said. "If you have an email address, I can send them to you."

"All right." The detective pulled out one of her cards and passed it across the desk to Denise. She pointed to the bottom of the card. "The email address is right here."

Denise glanced at the card and slid it into her top desk drawer. Then she stood up. "Now, you'll really have to excuse me. I'm going to be late for my meeting."

Officer Stanley stood up, too. Steady eye contact. "We'll be in touch," she said.

Patricia left Mid-Atlantic and headed back towards the police station. The traffic was slow, but she didn't mind. There was a lot to think about, and she wanted some uninterrupted time to do it. She was almost certain that Denise Bascomb was lying about something. Whatever she was doing in Chicago, she wasn't being honest about it. The only problem was motive. Why would Denise Bascomb want to kill Victor Wagner? She didn't know about the relationship between him and Ronald Clemons (or did she? Have to check whether she could have found out). And if she didn't, then she wouldn't even know Victor Wagner existed, let alone have a reason to kill him. And that would mean she didn't kill Clemons, unless there were two separate killers.

[235]

"I really don't see it," Luke shook his head. "It's too much of a coincidence that someone kills Ronald Clemons, and then someone else tries to kill his son. It's got to be the same person."

"Maybe," said Patricia. "But if you're right, and there's only one killer, then it's not Denise Bascomb."

"OK, so it isn't."

Patricia looked across her desk at Luke. He had a way of cutting to the chase like that. It was part of what she liked about working with him. And this time, he was right. So, it wasn't Denise Bascomb.

"All I'm saying," Luke went on, "is that we don't have a reason to think there are two killers. So, if Bascomb didn't try to kill Victor Wagner, then she probably didn't kill Ron Clemons. I'm not saying we ignore her."

"Good, because I'd like to know what she was really doing in Chicago."

"Or do you just not like her?"

Sometimes Luke's cutting to the chase could be uncomfortable.

"So, she's not on my Contacts list – wait!" Patricia nearly jumped out of her seat.

Luke put down the coffee mug he'd just picked up. "Are you OK?"

"Her phone contacts! Her calls!"

"Whose? Denise Bascomb's?"

"Yeah. Whatever she was doing in Chicago, she might have called people. They'd be on her list."

Luke nodded. "Yeah, they would. Can we get clearance to ask for her phone?"

"I'll talk to the boss about it." Patricia got all the way out of her seat this time and rushed towards Grant's office.

Lina smiled as she closed her email in-box. The websites and promotional pictures that Rachel had sent her looked fantastic. A visit to Napa was exactly what Rachel needed, and it would be very good for her to get away for a bit. Ron's death had hit her hard, and the police weren't making anything any easier. It would be a welcome relief to escape their incessant questioning. It was definitely the right idea to suggest that Rachel take a trip.

For now, though, there were other things to do. Kyle would be home in an hour and a half. That left Lina forty-five minutes to get some gardening done before she started dinner. She wanted to move a few of her perennials to that sunny spot by the corner of the house before the next rain came. She turned her computer off, then went out to the garage to get the trowel and her gardening gloves. That was another thing she was glad of: she'd gotten Rachel to pay some attention to her garden. The weather was getting warmer, and working outdoors was healthy. If it helped Rachel, so much the better.

Patricia sat across from her boss, waiting to hear what he'd have to say. There were only a few seconds of silence, but it felt like an eternity. Finally, Grant shook his head and said, "I don't know. You're not showing me motive. Denise Bascomb had no reason to want to kill Victor Wagner. That means we'd have two killers, and my gut's telling me that's not what happened."

Another minute of silence. Patricia dropped her eyes. Her gut was telling her the same thing. Then she raised them again. "But shouldn't we at least find out what she was doing in Chicago? She's been lying to us, and that makes me wonder about her."

"Me, too, but we have nothing to link her to the Wagner case. And I can't get a warrant for her phone records without something concrete."

"But –"

"You heard me, Stanley. We'll follow up that lead if we get a stronger connection between her and Wagner. For now, back off. You and Enders have plenty of other possibilities."

There wasn't much Patricia could say to that. She nodded, got up, and went back to her desk.

"So, what'd the boss say?" Luke asked.

Patricia pulled an imaginary lever and made a fake flushing noise. "Basically, the same thing you did. We don't have a motive, and we can't link her to the attempt on Wagner. So, it's a no-go for now."

"Doesn't mean we don't keep her in mind. Besides, it's not like there aren't other things to do. We haven't even checked into Lina Porter, for instance."

"You're right. But I still don't see where she has a motive."

"Even if she doesn't, if there's foxglove on her property, then Rachel Clemons could have access to it."

"You're right."

"Of course I am."

"Shut up."

Luke looked at Patricia a little more closely. "Don't beat yourself up," he said. "It wasn't a bad idea to check into that whole Chicago thing."

Luke was right on both counts. Patricia nodded, squared her shoulders a little, and pulled the case file towards her. For the next half hour, she flipped through the pages, trying to focus her thoughts. All they really had were some probably unreliable descriptions of a woman who'd met with both Clemons and Wagner on the days they were poisoned. And that wasn't much of anything. There were some motives, especially the wife and son. But without a better ID, there was no way to link anyone specific to the poison, and no way to prove anyone had had the opportunity to use it. They would have to find out if any of these people had foxglove. It was time to take a closer look at people's yards. Starting with Lina Porter's.

Greg Isaacson took a last glance around his office as he picked up his set of keys from where they had been lying next to the computer. He'd had a long, annoying day, and it wasn't made any easier by what was happening with Denise. He'd never thought of himself as stupid or gullible, but maybe he was, at least where she was concerned. There was just something about her. He shook his head to clear his mind. No more of that. He wasn't going to let her turn him inside out any more. He left his office, locking the door behind him, and went through the building and outside to the parking lot. He got into his Volkswagen and, nodding his head decisively, joined the homeward-bound traffic.

He thought of stopping at a florist's, but he wasn't in the mood for a romantic gesture. No, he'd go right over to Denise's place and talk to her again. He'd have to make her understand that she couldn't treat him that way – just telling him whatever she thought he wanted to hear. He took his time getting over there, so he could be sure she'd be home.

When he got to Denise's building, Greg parked the car and went to the door. He saw that it was opened just a little, and gave it a small push, calling out, "Denise? It's me." She didn't answer, but he could hear her voice in another room. She must be on the telephone. He walked all the way into the living room and sat down to wait until she finished her conversation.

"...can't be there until next week," she was saying. "I can stay three days, if that works...No... OK...All right, I'll call you when I've made the reservations. Yeah, see you in Chicago." Then she finished the call. She nearly dropped her telephone when she saw Greg.
"I didn't hear you come in," she gasped. "You scared the hell out of me!"
"Sorry, but you were on the phone, and I didn't want to interrupt."
"Look, Greg, this isn't a good time. I've got a million things to do."
Greg didn't move.
"Come on, Greg, I really need to get things done."
Finally, he spoke. "I heard you say something about Chicago. Are you going there?"
"Not that I'm required to report to you, but, yes, I'm going for a few days."
"We don't have any clients that far west."
"I'm hoping to change that." It was something in the way her eyes flicked just a little. Or maybe it was the way her shoulders moved.
"Bullshit," he said.

"Excuse me?"

"Bullshit."

"What's that supposed to mean?"

"We've never had clients in Illinois, and the company's never pushed to expand that far. Now, all of a sudden, you make two trips there within, what, a couple weeks? What's going on?"

"I'm trying to help the business grow, that's what. Is that suddenly a crime?"

Greg ran an impatient hand through his hair. "Trying to grow the business isn't a crime, and you know that's not what's bothering me. Not telling me the truth is what's bothering me."

"So now you're calling me a liar?" Denise stepped closer to him, leaning forward as she did.

Greg stood up. "I don't know what to believe any more. You tell the police one thing, you tell me another. What do you expect me to think?"

Denise took a deep breath. There it was again. That eye shift. Something in way she held herself. "Why is it such a big problem for you if I go to Chicago for a couple of days?"

Greg shook his head. "Don't put this on me. If you go to Chicago, that's your business. But don't lie to me about things and then expect me to take it like a good little boy."

"I'm not lying to –"

Greg put his hand up, palm towards Denise. "Save it, OK? I'm going now." He turned and went out. Denise could hear his footsteps as he walked to his car. A minute later, she heard the engine start.

The traffic wasn't too bad as Patricia got into her Honda. She was glad that she'd been able to get out of the station on time today, since she had an appointment with Dr. Zara. So far, she hadn't told Luke, or Grant, for that matter, about those appointments. Not that either of them would judge her – well, she hoped not – but there was still something about getting mental health care that made people uneasy. She tried to clear her mind as she headed towards Dr. Zara's office. "What would you like to talk about?" would be Zara's first question, and Patricia had no idea yet what her answer would be.

By the time she'd gotten to the building where Dr. Zara had her office, though, Patricia felt ready. She parked her car, and within a few minutes was waiting in the reception area. After a moment or two, Dr. Zara opened her office door, came out, and said, "You ready for me?"
Patricia nodded, smiled, and got up to follow Dr. Zara back into her office. After they were both seated came the inevitable question.
"What do you want to talk about today?"
"I've been thinking about that. It's – I guess Becky. I mean me and Becky. She's not the problem."
"OK, let's talk about you and Becky."
"We had a fight. It wasn't a huge thing, and I think we're past it. But it scared me."
"Why?"
"I don't want to lose her."
"Did you?"
"No, but still."
"A lot of couples argue. It's part of being close to someone. But a lot of couples stay together. An argument – even a serious one – doesn't mean you'll break up."
"I know, but...."

For the next forty minutes, Patricia and Dr. Zara worked together. By the end of the session, Patricia felt less anxious about Becky. She really did want them to stay together, maybe even someday get married. But that wasn't today's problem. She glanced around the office as she got ready to leave. "I didn't notice that when I came in," she said, pointing to a plant on the desk. "It's nice."

"Thanks. It's a spider plant."

Patricia took a closer look at it as she stood up. "That reminds me," she said half to herself.

"Of what?"

"Just a lead I have to follow up on for this case I'm working on."

Patricia got back to the police station within a few minutes and made a beeline for her desk. She sent a quick text to Becky: *Gonna be a little late. CU as soon as I can.* Then, she started riffling through the papers on her desk. With a satisfied "a-*ha,*" she grabbed the one she wanted, shoving the rest aside. She read it over, nodded to herself, and then logged on to her computer.

"You still here?" Luke asked as he came back from the men's room.

"Yeah, we need to look more closely at some of these people's homes."

It only took Luke a second. "We do need to do that." He moved his chair around so that he could look at Patricia's computer screen. On it was a list of the people they'd interviewed.

"What's your plan?"

"Let's start with Lina Porter's home. She gardens."

"People can buy that stuff without actually having a garden. Didn't you tell me they sell it in garden stores?"

"I know, but people who don't do any gardening might not think of using foxglove."

Patricia and Luke spent the next twenty minutes putting together the addresses of the people on their list. Then they went over the list again. Trent Rakins, Wade Messner, and Ron (well, Rachel) Clemons all had houses and yards, and probably gardens. And wait, so did Lina Porter. Patricia still didn't see where she had motive, but it was worth a check. Emma Yeats lived in an apartment. So did Greg Isaacson. They'd already checked Denise Bascomb's place and hadn't seen any foxglove. It wasn't a sure thing. After all, you could grow a plant on a balcony or windowsill. But it was a start.

Thirteen

"You've really come at a bad time, Officer. I'm just leaving for work." Lina Porter stood blocking the door, daring the two police officers to make her late.

"We'll only be a few minutes, Mrs. Porter," Patricia said. "We're following up on a few questions we have about your brother-in-law's murder."

"But why come back here? I didn't have anything to do with that."

"We just have one or two questions."

"Well?"

"Did you see Rachel or Ronald Clemons on the day he died?" Patricia asked.

"No, that was a weekday. I was at work and didn't know anything had happened until Rachel called and told me."

Patricia made a note and looked up from what she'd written. "And what time was that?"

"Around ten, I think."

"When was the last time you saw Mr. Clemons?"

"A couple of days earlier. Look, I really need to get to work now."

"I'll walk you to your car. Thanks for your time." As they walked towards the car, Patricia glanced around. "You do have a nice garden."

"It's not bad. I don't have the time to do what I'd like with it." She opened her car door, and nodded slightly as she got in. Patricia gave a brief wave as Lina pulled away.

Once the car was gone, Patricia took a short walk around the front of the property. No foxglove anywhere. She hadn't lied; the Porters did have a nice yard with attractive lowers and bushes. And some patches that looked ready for planting. But no foxglove. The back yard was enclosed, and the gate to it was locked. But Patricia could just see over it. She didn't see any foxglove there, either.

Rachel looked out the window at the dull, leaden sky. It was raw outside today, and she hugged herself against the chill, even though she was inside. In less than a week, though, she'd be in Napa, where the weather was a lot better. It wouldn't change anything, really. Ron was still dead, would always be dead. But getting away was a good idea. She had to give Lina credit for that one. Those police detectives had told her to let them know if she was going anywhere. Well, that could wait. She had no desire to talk to those –
Ding dong!
Rachel glanced at her watch. Lina was at work, and she wouldn't come to the front door, anyway. It was probably either someone selling something or a religious evangelist. As she made her way downstairs, Rachel steeled herself to get rid of whoever was trying to sell something or convert her.

"Hello, Mrs. Clemons. If you have a few minutes, we have a few more questions." God, would they never leave her alone?
"Come in," she said, in what she hoped was an ungracious tone of voice. It was that young man again. He was with the older one – Grant, that was his name. Rachel hoped Grant would do the talking. He did.

"We just have a few follow-up questions," Grant said as he and the other one followed Rachel into the living room.

"What questions? I've told you everything I know."

"We'd just like to go over some things one more time – just to make sure we have it all down."

"All right." Should she tell them she was in a hurry? No, better not say anything. She thought of her suitcase lying open on her bed. Well, they hadn't told her she couldn't go anywhere. Still, best not to go into that.

The young man – Enders, that was it – glanced out the living room window. "Looks like you've been doing some work in your front garden."

"Some," Rachel nodded. "Not today, though."

"What do you grow?"

"Irises, daylilies, some phlox. A few other things. My sister Lina convinced me to spend more time in the garden. I'm liking it now that the weather's getting a little warmer. But wait, you didn't come here to talk about my gardening, did you?"

"No, I just couldn't help noticing." That's right. He'd said something about the garden last time. She'd forgotten.

Grant took over. "You told us that you last saw your husband on the morning of his death, right?"

"That's right. It was about seven-thirty or so. Then he left. I didn't see him again until, well, until after."

"And he didn't say anything about meeting anyone before he went to the office?"

"No, I mean, I think he usually met with the staff when he got to the office. But not before."

Grant leaned forward. "Do you know a local place called 'A Taste of Home?'"

What was this supposed to mean? "Ron sometimes stopped there on the way to work. Why?"
"It looks like he stopped there that last morning, too. Did you know that?"
Rachel shook her head. "He didn't report to me. But it wasn't unusual for him."
"So you wouldn't know if he met anyone there?"
Rachel shook her head again.

After a few more questions, they finally left. It hadn't been too bad, really, Rachel thought. Just about whether Ron went to A Taste of Home. Nothing else. He used to like that place, and the police probably heard that already from Emma Yeats or someone else at the office. It could've been a lot worse.

Grant and Enders fastened their safety belts and Enders started the police unit's motor. "What did you think?" Grant asked. That was Luke's cue to show he could draw conclusions.
"I don't think she knew what we were really looking for," Luke said slowly. "There was no foxglove last time, and I didn't see any this time, either."
"She could still –"
"Yeah, she could. And she's the widow. But still..." Luke nodded.
 "We'll see how Stanley does with..."

...Trent Rakins. That was the next name on the list. Patricia didn't really want to talk to him; she found his glib manner annoying. Besides, that fake cheerfulness made her wonder how much she could trust what he said. Probably not much. But that didn't mean he was a murderer. She was going to have to get better at not letting her feelings about these people get in the way.

For now, she put a check mark next to Rakins' name and input his address to the police car's GPS unit. A second later, a map of the area popped up, and Patricia pushed the 'Directions' option on the system. As she turned the motor on, the GPS' voice intoned, *Head east for half a mile, then turn left.* It only took ten minutes to get to Rakins' home. As she pulled up to the driveway, Patricia could see that it was a well-kept property. He (or whoever he paid) obviously cared about it. A minute later and she was parked.

"Thanks for coming out this far." Rakins was waiting for her at the front door.

"Not a problem. Thanks for talking to me outside of work hours."

"Come on in.'

Patricia thanked Rakins and followed him into a small, but expensive-looking, living room. "Have a seat. Would you like some coffee? Something stronger? I think the sun's going down." He chuckled as he said it.

"No, thanks."

"Well, now, what can I do you for?"

"I just have a few follow-up questions."

"Shoot."

Patricia pulled a small notebook out of her pocket and flipped through it. "You told us that, on the morning that Mr. Clemons died, you had a client meeting. Is that right?"

"Yes, that's right."

"So you weren't at that morning's staff meeting?"

[249]

"No, I wasn't. I think I already told you people all of this." Rakins' tone got a little sharper.

"I know. We just have to go back over these things – just to make sure we have our facts right."

Rakins relaxed a bit. "Sure, I understand."

Good, Patricia thought. He remembered that it's not a smart idea to annoy the police. She nodded and went back to the notebook. "The thing is, though, that you were listed as being at that staff meeting."

Rakins leaned back a bit and templed his fingers. "Hmm...that is odd." After a second, he snapped his fingers. A trace of the bonded, veneered smile returned. "You know what it might be? I'm usually at those meetings. Maybe Emma went on auto-pilot and just listed my name."

"That could be." Might as well make him think he was right. It could get him to open up a little. "Do you happen to remember the name of the client you were visiting that morning?"

"I can't be a hundred percent sure without checking with Max – Max Anselm, my assistant – but I think my appointment was with the Wingate people. They sell top-of-the-line homes, and we've been working with them on publicity."

Patricia made a few notes, and then looked up. "Thanks, I think that's all I need for right now."

She and Rakins both got up and he walked her to the door. When they got outside, she looked around the neatly-kept property. "You have a nice yard."

"Thanks, you should see it when it's nicer outside. We have a company that comes in."

"They do a good job."

"I have to admit," with a little self-deprecatory laugh, "I don't know a whole lot about gardening.

Fortunately, there are some good landscaping places in the area."

"What company do you use?"

"Forever Green is the name."

Patricia made a note, thanked him for his time, and walked back to her car. Rakins stood on his porch, watching her as she left.

Wade Messner heard the door buzzer from the small kitchen where he was pouring himself a whisky. He put the glass down, crossed through the living room and glanced through the door's peephole. It was that police officer he'd seen at the office. What the hell did she want?

"Can I help you?" he asked as he opened the door.

"I just a have one or two questions about Mr. Clemons' death,' the woman said. "Can we talk for a few minutes?"

"Uh, yeah, sure, come in." It was definitely better not to seem uncooperative.

"Thanks."

Wade showed the detective – she said her name was Detective Stanley – into his living room and offered her a seat on one of the two Laz-E-Boy recliners.

"Can I get you something? Coffee? Tea?"

"I'm fine, thanks. I won't take up much of your time."

Wade sat down in the other recliner. "I thought you people were going to arrest Trent Rakins. I'm surprised you haven't."

"Nobody's under arrest yet. Right now, we're trying to get all the information we can. You can help us."

Wade sat up a little straighter. "Well, of course I'll help if I can."

"Great. Now, you were at the staff meeting on the morning of Mr. Clemons' death, right?"

"That's right. I saw him at our staff meeting that morning. But I didn't speak to him after the meeting, and I didn't see him again. But I know Rakins did."

"Did you see Mr. Clemons before the staff meeting?"

"I don't remember for sure, but I don't think so. I usually go right to my office when I get in, and I don't see much of anyone before our meetings."

"And after the meeting?"

"Like I said, I didn't see Ron again. I had another meeting, and I had to get ready for it, so I left right away. But I did see him talking to Trent Rakins."

"We'll check into that."

"I hope you do. If anyone had a reason to kill Ron, he did."

"You mentioned that before. Can you tell me more about it?"

"Well – and I think I told you people about this already – Ron built up the business to be top-of-the-line. A real boutique sort of company. Trent wants to change all that and go for, well, lower-end clients."

"And Mr. Clemons knew this?"

"I'm pretty sure he did. And I wouldn't be surprised at all if they argued about it. The company's reputation was everything to Ron. And Trent just wants to flush it all down the toilet." Wade took a breath. He needed to sound a little more reasonable. "Well, at least that's how I see it."

"So, Mr. Clemons and Mr. Rakins didn't get along?"

"Not really."

"But you agreed with Mr. Clemons about the company's direction?"

"Absolutely. We need to keep our exclusive image. Otherwise, we'll lose the clients we do have, and we won't get well-paying new ones."

"And you've spoken to Mr. Rakins about this?"

"Of course I have. But he doesn't listen to anyone's opinion but his own. He's a bully that way."

Detective Stanley nodded and made some more notes. Then she stood up. "I won't keep you any more. I appreciate what you've told me."

Wade stood up, too. "I'm happy to do whatever I can to help." He walked with her to the door. As they stepped outside, she said, "You've got a nice front garden here."

It was nice of her to notice. "Thanks," he said. "I wish I could spend more time in my garden, to be honest. But, you know – work and all that."

"Of course. Do you have a back garden, too?"

"Just some shrubs and a few other perennials. Nothing fancy. Um – would you like to see?"

"Sure, that'd be nice."

They walked around behind Wade's small, one-story house and he showed her some rhododendron and lilacs. "They're not quite at their best yet," he said apologetically. "But it's getting warmer. They'll come out soon."

"I'm sure they'll be great," she said. "Thanks for showing me around."

They went back to the front of the house, where Wade watched her get into her car.

Strike two, Patricia thought as she started her motor. She hadn't seen anything that looked like foxglove. Of course, that didn't mean he didn't know about it

[253]

and couldn't use it. Or that he couldn't have dug it up after the fact and replaced it with something more innocuous. The problem was motive. Why would he kill Clemons? They didn't have any work disputes, and they didn't seem to be connected outside of work.

"Maybe Rakins wasn't the only one bullying him," Luke said. Patricia had gotten back to the police station a few minutes earlier. Now they were comparing notes about their interviews.
 "What do you mean?" Patricia put down the bottle of water she was drinking and looked across at Luke.
"Well, he really dislikes Rakins. Can't say I'm a fan, myself. But anyway, there's a reason for that."
"OK, so they have different ideas for what the company should do."
"Yeah, but it's more than that. When we talked to Messner the first time, he was just coming out of Rakins' office. He was fuming about something, and it seemed like more than just a work disagreement."
"So, he doesn't like Rakins. You just said you don't, either."
"No, I swear this was more than that. Hear me out. Say the reason he hates Rakins is that Rakins is a bully."
"Go on"
"All right, so what if Messner is the company target? You know, everyone picks on him. What if Clemons did, too? He might lash out."

Patricia shook her head. "I don't know. Do you use poison to lash out at a bully?"
"You could."

"Yeah, but I just don't see him that way. I know, I know!" She put up a hand as Luke opened his mouth. "We can't rule anyone out. I'm just saying."

"Whatever." Luke shrugged. "It's something to think about, that's all."

"Have you talked to the boss about it?" Patricia tried to mend fences.

"Not yet. It just hit me."

"We could see what he says, anyway."

"Yeah." Luke looked mollified. Good. No need to alienate your partner without a damned good reason. Besides, Luke could be right. Patricia hadn't thought about the whole bullying angle. That was the problem with learning to be a detective – figuring out when to hold your ground and when to keep an open mind.

Patricia started to look through her work email. She was interrupted about three minutes later.

"I'm glad you two are here." Patricia and Luke both looked up. Dominique Reeves, the daytime receptionist, was standing in front of them. "There's someone here who wants to see you. Says his name is Greg Isaacson."

"Thanks, Dominique," Luke said. "Did he say which of us he wants to see?"

"He just said he wants to talk to the people working on Ron Clemons' death."

Patricia and Luke looked at each other. "We'll be there in a minute," Luke said.

"Wonder what he wants," Patricia said when Dominique left.

"We're about to find out."

This wasn't an interrogation, but neither Patricia nor Luke wanted to do anything wrong. "How about you fill Grant in, and I'll find a room to talk to our guy," Patricia said as they stood up. Luke nodded and they went their separate ways.

"Thanks for coming in," Patricia extended her hand as Greg Isaacson rose from the chair he'd been using. Isaacson shook her hand absently and glanced around a few times. "Let's find a place to sit down and talk." Isaacson nodded and followed her silently.

When they got to the larger of the station's interview rooms, Patricia opened the door and showed Isaacson in. "It's not exactly luxurious, but it is private," she explained as they went in. "Can I get you some water? A soda?"
"I'm fine, thanks. I – this won't take long, will it?"
Patricia tried to stall for time. Where was Luke?
"My partner will be here in a minute. For now, how about you let me know how we can help you and we'll go from there, OK?"
Isaacson nodded again. "All right. It's about –"
The door opened and Luke came in. He gave Patricia a brief nod and sat down. Patricia gave him a slight smile and a nod. "OK, I think we're ready."
"All right," Isaacson said again. "It's about Denise – Denise Bascomb. She and I – well, you know we've been seeing each other. I think something might be going on with her."
"I'm not sure what you mean," Patricia said.
"I found out she's going to Chicago for a few days."
Isaacson started to get a little more comfortable. "No big deal, right? People go to Chicago all the time. But she wouldn't tell me why – well, she gave me an excuse, but I don't think she was telling the truth."

"And you think this has something to do with Mr. Clemons' death?" Trust Luke to get to the point. "That's the thing. I don't know. All I know is, she was here in town when Ron was killed. And she was in Chicago that other time – that attempted murder you asked us about. And now she's going to Chicago again, and she's not being honest about why."

"We'll follow up with that, Mr. Isaacson," Patricia made a note on the pad she'd remembered to bring. "Is there anything else you think we should know?" Isaacson shook his head. "I don't think so. And this could be nothing. It might be all in my head. But I just have a feeling it's not."

Luke said, "We're glad you came in." Then all three got up, and Luke showed Isaacson out.

When he got back to his desk, he saw that Patricia was looking at the notes she'd made. "So what do you think?" he asked.

"I think it's weird that she's not being open about what she's been doing in Chicago," Patricia answered. "But it could be innocent. And besides, we still can't connect her with Victor Wagner. Without that, there's no reason for her to try to kill him. It just doesn't make sense. I want to talk to her again."

"Definitely."

"I want to get the OK to check her telephone records, too. If there's a link to Chicago or Palatine, that might be interesting."

As they sat back down at their desks, Patricia asked, "What did Grant say about your theory? Did you talk to him about it?"

Luke shrugged. "I mentioned it. He said we could talk about it. But we'd need to find out whether Messner was being bullied, and whether Clemons was involved. And that could take some time."

Time! Patricia looked at the time on her telephone – nearly six. And she'd told Becky that morning that she'd try to be home at a decent hour tonight. "You mind if I take off?" she asked Luke. "We can start talking to people about that tomorrow."
"Yeah, that works. I was thinking about leaving myself. The boss told me he's in a meeting for the rest of the day, and he wants to talk to us in the morning. Seems like a good time to wrap it up."
"OK, see you tomorrow, then."
"Hi to Becky."
"Yup."

Even with the slow traffic, Patricia still got home before six-thirty. She smiled a little to herself as she got her things together. Becky would be glad she'd remembered her promise. She took three deep breaths ("Try to let go of work when you get out of your car," Dr. Zara had advised. "Don't carry your baggage with you.") and headed to the apartment. Then she went inside.

Becky was sitting on the living room sofa, going through the day's mail. "Nothing much," she said, holding up the papers in her hand, "unless you have a burning desire to save 20% on towels at Bed, Bath & Beyond."
"Nope," Patricia plopped down on the sofa beside Becky. They hugged, and Patricia asked, "How was your day?"
"OK, just hectic. I'm wiped. Yours?"

"Same."

"Hm… I prescribe a mindless movie and some pizza."

"Add in some beer and you've got a deal."

"You got it."

Becky started to get up from the sofa, but Patricia held onto her hand. "What?" she smiled.

"It's just – I don't know what I'd do without you. You're amazing."

"You'd be in the gutter is what you'd do," Becky laughed a little as she gently pulled her hand free.

"Yeah, probably. I just don't want you to think I don't appreciate you, that's all." Patricia watched as Becky got up to deal with dinner. She could imagine them twenty, thirty, forty years from now. Dr. Zara had told her she would keep healing. Maybe this was part of it.

Fourteen

"So you really think it might be a workplace bullying thing?" Grant leaned back in his chair and templed his fingers as he listened.

"I don't know for sure," Luke hesitated a bit. "But like I said yesterday, I know that Wade Messner hates Trent Rakins."

"So?"

Patricia almost winced in sympathy. Grant could make you feel like a complete idiot with one word when he wanted to.

"So, I'm pretty sure it's because Rakins is bullying Messner."

"All right. Let's say he is. Where does that leave us?"

"I know this a leap," Luke admitted. "But what if Clemons was a bully too? If he targeted Messner, then that would be a motive, wouldn't it?"

Grant leaned forward, wearing his 'teachable moment' expression. "A theory is only as good as what it explains. So, let's see what we have. Let's say there's a culture of bullying at Mid-Atlantic. Let's say it came from the top – from Ron Clemons. OK so far. For whatever reason, Messner was the target. Also fits in. He's angry, he lashes out, and kills Clemons. You never know what someone who's been bullied might do, so OK. But what about Victor Wagner?"

Luke was quiet for a moment. Then he said, "I see what you mean. But what if Wagner and Clemons are two separate things completely – not linked?"

Grant sat back in his chair. Patricia and Luke waited while he gathered his thoughts. "Is it possible?' he finally said. "Yeah, it could be. But I don't think so, and I don't think you two do, either. Too many coincidences for it to be two different people."

"And if it is the same person," Luke admitted, "Why would Messner want to kill Victor Wagner?"

"Exactly," Grant nodded. Then, seeing Luke's facial expression, he added, "But if you find anything that links Messner to Wagner, that's a different thing. Let me know."

"I will."

"What else do we have?"

"Denise Bascomb." And Patricia detailed Greg Isaacson's visit to them.

Grant nodded slowly. "Fair enough. Something funny might be going on. Go ahead and ask a few questions. That's it. For now, no warrants, even for telephone records."

"But –"

Grant silenced Patricia with one look. "But we run into Victor Wagner again. There's nothing that says she knew him. She might have wanted to kill Clemons, but not Wagner. Look," he added, glancing at both Patricia and Luke. "Let's not make this more complicated than it has to be unless we need to do that. If this is all connected, then we're looking at one person. And that one person has to have had a motive for wanting both Clemons and his son dead. So, we find someone with connections to both men. If we get a really good reason to make this into two cases, we'll talk about that then. Got it?"

Patricia and Luke took their cue and left.

When they got back to their desks, Patricia said, "The bullying thing - it wasn't a bad idea."

"Save it," Luke put a hand up. "Please. I'm not in the fucking mood right now."

"Whatever," Patricia muttered. She rolled her eyes, put up her own hands, and sat down at her desk. Hopefully Luke would cool down soon. For now, she decided to start following up on what Greg Isaacson had told them. She didn't want to say anything to Luke about it right now, but they were going to need to follow up with Denise Bascomb. Her story left too much open.

Lina didn't usually take a full hour for her lunch, although she was entitled to it. Most of the time, she brought her lunch from home, or picked something up from a grocery store on the way in to work. But today, she wanted some extra time. She wanted to get some things for Rachel for her trip. Besides, she wanted a few things of her own. She turned off her computer, pushed her desk chair away from the desk, and picked up her telephone and handbag. Fortunately, Eagle Village was less than fifteen minutes from her office. And at this time of day, the roads weren't likely to be crowded. The trip would cost her plenty, but it was a nice place, and the shops had some beautiful clothes.

Rachel put her telephone down on the desk next to her computer. She bit her lower lip as she tried to figure out how she was going to answer Lina's text. The day after tomorrow, she'd be leaving for Napa, and there was still a lot to do. She wanted time to organize everything, take care of her clients, and finish her packing, and she wanted to do it by herself. But she knew Lina well enough to know that she wouldn't take 'no' for an answer. And it would be better to have Lina visit this evening than

tomorrow. After a moment, she picked her telephone up again and texted back:
That'll work. About 7?

A minute later, she got her answer:

OK. I'll bring Chinese.

Rachel almost asked if Kyle would be coming along, but then she remembered he had some sort of business trip. Lina had said he wouldn't be back for a week. She glanced at the time on her computer: 3:30. She'd better get a move on and go over her client accounts if she was going to be spending the evening with Lina.

"But I've already explained the whole thing to you," Denise Bascomb sighed. With the same tone of voice that you might use to repeat your order to a trainee coffee barista, she went on. "I was at a trade show in Chicago. I met some people there who work for Peerless. They wanted to talk to me about a position. It was informal and didn't go anywhere. End of story. What more can I say?"
"That's the thing," Patricia said. "We haven't been able to find anyone at Peerless who talked to you about a job."

Denise shifted a little on the living room sofa where she was sitting. Patricia had gotten the green light from Grant to follow up on Denise's story, and she'd decided it was best to try to talk to her at home. Remembering Grant's warning not to complicate things, she wouldn't push too hard. But she did want answers. She took advantage of the silence as Denise shifted again. "I don't know what else you want me to tell you."

Patricia leaned forward slightly, propping her forearms on her knees. "Look. We're trying to find out who killed Ronald Clemons. Anything else is less important. And anything private stays that way unless it has to do with the murder."

Denise shook her head. "It doesn't," she finally said.

Patricia sat up straighter. This was going to be tricky. Should she ask a question, or stay silent? Hopefully she'd get better at this over time. For now, she decided to wait for just a minute more. When nothing happened, she reached into a pocket and pulled out a notebook and small pen. At least she'd remembered those. Denise seemed to see that she wasn't going to get away with saying nothing. After a moment, she sighed.

"All right. I've been holding back a little. Just a little," she added when she saw Patricia's face. "I've been taking advantage of a business opportunity there. I haven't said anything about it at work, but that's what I've been doing."

"I'm going to need more details."

Denise nodded. "There are a lot of politicians out there who need to polish up their images. I mean, nobody's perfect, right? So, they get help from publicity people like me. It's a big business, actually."

"And you've been image-polishing?"

"Exactly" Denise half-smiled.

Patricia looked down at her notepad again. "I'm going to need your client's name and contact information."

Denise looked away and then back at Patricia. "I guess you can't take my word for it, can you?" Patricia shook her head. Then, Denise pulled her telephone out of her pocket and swiped the screen to unlock it. She scrolled through her Contacts list, and then passed the telephone to Patricia. "Scott Donaldson," she said. "He's an Illinois state senator from Chicago. He's looking towards a national career, though – wants to go to Washington. So, I'm helping his team with optics and some publicity." Patricia couldn't resist asking. "Any skeletons in the closet?"

A raised eyebrow. "A couple of financial things. Nothing we can't handle. No murders, anyway." Patricia made a note of Donaldson's contact information and returned the telephone.

Now came the obvious question. "Why didn't you tell us all of this from the beginning?"

"I have an exclusivity contract." Denise looked at Patricia to be sure she understood. She did. Then Denise continued. "This kind of publicity isn't exactly the same sort of work I do at Mid-Atlantic, but it's close enough that I could get in real trouble. I couldn't tell anyone, or word might get around." The next question was going to be awkward. "Greg Isaacson doesn't know, then?"

"No – well, I've never said anything to him. He'd understand, I know he would. But keep his mouth shut? I'm less sure of that. Besides," a little too quickly, "I don't want to put Greg in an awkward position." Then, she looked up sharply at Patricia. "You're not going to tell him, are you?" Patricia closed her notebook and put it in the pocket of her khakis. "I can't guarantee anything," she answered truthfully. Then, she saw Denise's expression. "But I don't see any reason we should have to." Denise nodded and sat back, visibly more relaxed. Then she looked at the elegant black leather watch she was wearing. "I'm supposed to meet some clients for dinner," she said, "And I'd like to shower and change before I do. Do you have any more questions?"

"Not now,' Patricia stood up to leave. "We'll be in touch if anything else comes up." She felt Denise watching her as she left.

Steam puffed out from the boxes of chicken lo mein and rice as Lina opened them. Rachel didn't feel much like eating, but the food did smell good. And Lina'd remembered that Rachel didn't like egg rolls. She'd brought cream cheese won tons instead. Rachel put out napkins and poured glasses of sauvignon blanc. When everything was ready, they both sat at the kitchen table. Lina took a sip of her wine. "So, are you all packed?" she asked.

"Almost. Just a few last-minute things to go." After a second, Rachel added, "And thanks for the dress and hat. They're great." She lifted her own glass and took a swallow.

"It'll be good for you to get away," Lina nodded decisively. "And I don't want you to even think about anything here while you're gone. I'll stop by to get your mail and make sure the house is OK." That was nice of Lina. Rachel smiled a little and said "I appreciate it. And it will be nice to take some time away. I need it right now."

"'Course you do." Lina didn't know how right she was. Or that she was part of the reason Rachel wanted a break. "Now, let's open up this food while it's hot."

Rachel nodded. She wanted to change the subject, anyway. She should have known better. There wasn't much conversation for the next few minutes, but then, Lina asked, "Are you flying direct to Napa?"

"No, it's a whole lot cheaper to fly into San Francisco and rent a car from there. It's only an hour's drive."

"That makes sense," Lina agreed. "You want me to drive you to the airport in the morning?"

"No," a moment's hesitation. "Thanks. You have to work. I've already booked a shuttle, anyway."

"Well, if you're sure…"

"I am. Don't worry. So, when does Kyle get back from his trip?" That was enough to get Lina focused on something else, and for the rest of the meal, she and Rachel talked about Kyle (It's nice to have the place to yourself sometimes), about Lina's garden (I hope we get a few sunny days in a row – we need it), and about Rachel's business (You know, you really ought to think about doing some more online advertising).

When they were finished, Rachel put the leftover food back into the cartons and pushed them gently across the table towards Lina. "You take them," she insisted. "I'm leaving in the morning, and I'm not eating Chinese food for breakfast." For once, Lina didn't argue with her.

You sure you don't need anything?" she asked one last time.

"I'll be fine."

The sisters hugged, and Lina said, "Call me if you need me. It doesn't matter what time it is."

When Lina had finally gone, Rachel did the little bit
of cleaning that needed to be done in the kitchen
and started the dishwasher. Then she went upstairs
to finish her packing. Before long, she'd be in Napa.
Putting her things into the suitcase made it seem
more real to her. She even let herself think about
how it might be to stay there if she liked it well
enough. She could make those kinds of plans now.
Ron would have – but it didn't matter what Ron
would want any more. That was going to take some
getting used to. She blinked a few times,
swallowed, and finished putting what she could into
the suitcase. She'd do her toiletries in the morning.

Luke Enders sat upright in bed, breathing hard.
Whatever he'd been dreaming, it had been enough
to wake him up. Something about flowers, of all
things. He picked up his telephone and looked at the
time – 2:45am. What the hell had he been
dreaming? He knew it was important somehow. But
flowers? No, not flowers, gardens. Why would he
be thinking of plants and gardens? He didn't know
what it was, but something had gotten his attention.

Now, Luke got out of bed, glad that Gabrielle
hadn't spent the night last night, much as he loved
having her around. He wouldn't have wanted to
wake her. He stood looking out of his bedroom
window for a minute, but he didn't see anything
unusual. No, it hadn't been a noise. It was definitely
a dream. He lay back down in bed, stretched his
legs, and folded his arms under his head, trying to
think. Plants. Gardens. What was it? All he knew
was, it mattered.
Ten minutes later it came to him. He sat bolt
upright, practically jumped out of bed, and grabbed

[268]

his telephone. It was 3:15, and much too early to call anyone if it wasn't an emergency. But he had to talk his idea out with somebody. He was just going to have to risk being annoying.

U up? Patricia blinked and read the text with bleary eyes. This better be good. If it was Luke's idea of a joke, he was going to be in for it.
She texted back. *I am now. WTF? It's not even 3:30!*
I know. Sorry. It's about the Clemons case. Can u talk?
Call me in five, so I can move to another room.
K

Patricia eased out of the bedroom, happy to see that Becky had slept through the text sound. She went into the kitchen and, yawning deeply, poured herself a glass of orange juice. A minute later her telephone sounded.
"Hey, what's going on?" she asked as she sat down on a kitchen chair.
"I'm sorry I woke you up. Something just hit me, and it wouldn't let go. It's something we hadn't thought of yet, and I feel like it might be worth it."
"OK, what is it?" Couldn't an idea for the investigation wait until the sun rose, anyway?
"It's the soil."
"The what?"
"The soil at Lina Porter's house. You know, those patches that you said weren't planted with anything."
"Hold on, let me get my stuff." Patricia went to get her notebook. Two minutes later she was back.
"OK, I'm back."

"I'm just saying we should check them out. I mean what if there are seeds or something in them?"

"You're right about that," Patricia said slowly. "But why would Lina Porter kill her brother-in-law?"

"Could have been all kinds of reasons. We just don't know."

"You have a point. We can start on that when we get into the office."

Luke nodded, even though he knew Patricia couldn't see him. "OK, see you then. Grant is gonna like this."

"Not at four o'clock in the morning he won't. We'll tell him when we get in."

"Yup."

Now it was Patricia who couldn't sleep. She still had two hours before it was time to get up, but she was too restless to lie down and close her eyes. She went into the living room, sat on the sofa, and flipped through her notebook again. Lina Porter? Well, for one thing, she didn't have an obvious motive, and Grant had wanted them to start with the people who did. Fair enough, but Lina could easily get foxglove. And, unless there was a history nobody knew about, Ronald Clemons would have trusted her – would have eaten or drunk anything she gave him. It was just the question of motive. And seeing if they could actually link her to the foxglove.

And then there was the attempted murder in Palatine. If it was connected to Clemons' death, then Lina Porter would have to have been in that area. But nobody had bothered to find out if she was. *Damnit!* Patricia tossed her notebook down. How the *hell* could they have missed that?

"Don't be too hard on yourself," Grant said. It was almost four hours later, and he was sitting at his desk, across from Patricia and Luke. "We all missed seeing if she went to Chicago. That's why all three of us keep going over things until they make some sense."

"But I should have –" Patricia started.

"Stop it. Now. 'Shouldas' aren't going to get you anywhere. And they won't be helpful. We have a new angle now, so let's just follow it up. Enders, I want you to go visit Lina Porter. Find out what you can. Stanley, I'll try to get the OKs to get her records. We don't have much of a case, to be honest, so I'm not optimistic. But maybe we'll catch a break and find a judge in a good mood. Now, get out of here, both of you."

Luke and Patricia didn't need to be told twice.

While Patricia waited to hear whether she'd be allowed to request records, she decided to do a little more background checking. Nothing came up in the basic search – no arrests, no calls to the residence, no nothing. Even the Motor Vehicle Report came back clean. Lina Porter had obviously not had a lot of contact with the police. Still, that didn't mean she hadn't killed Clemons, and tried to kill his son. She did more searching, but she didn't find anything useful in the public or police databases. Maybe this whole thing was a waste of time.

Luke pulled up to Lina Porter's home. He didn't see any cars, and nobody answered when he rang the bell. Without a warrant, he couldn't search the house, but he took a look around before he left. Patricia'd been right. There was no foxglove growing in the front, and the gate between the front and the back yards was locked. He muttered a few curses, went back to his car, and called Patricia. Maybe she'd be able to tell him where Lina worked. She couldn't, but she did give him Rachel Clemons' address and telephone. That was better than nothing.

Fifteen minutes of traffic later, Luke found that Rachel Clemons wasn't home, either. He knew she worked out of her home, so he waited for a few minutes to see if she'd turn up. No such luck. He tried calling her, but his call went to voice mail. He left a message, waited ten more minutes, and went back to the station.

Luke and Grant got to Patricia's desk at almost the same moment. Luke sat down at his own desk, and Grant sat in one of the extra chairs. Neither looked happy.

"So, what's the story?" Patricia asked. Luke waited for Grant to start.

"I just got off the phone. We're not going to get the go-ahead for any searches or warrants right now. At least not on Lina Porter. It's just like I thought – we don't have anything solid. Mostly, we don't have a motive. We're going to need more."

Luke blew his breath out. "And I couldn't even talk to her. When I got to her house, she wasn't home. Neither was Rachel Clemons. She didn't pick up, either, when I called."

Grant nodded. "Do we have a telephone number or place of employment for Lina Porter?"

"Not yet," Patricia said. Why hadn't she thought of that?

"Well, get them. We need to talk to her. If you have to, go to her work site and talk to her there."

"Got it," Patricia and Luke said at the same time.

Thank God for social media, Patricia thought. It didn't take long to find Lina Porter's telephone number. She called it, but all she got was voice mail. She left a message and went back to searching. It only took a few more minutes on Facebook to find out that Lina Porter worked at Tredyffrin Township Parks and Recreation, but when she called the place, Lina didn't answer her telephone. Patricia left a message when that call went to voice mail, too, and then hung up. She sat for a moment, tapping her index finger on her desk. Then, on impulse, she called back. This time, she pushed 'O' to be connected to the receptionist. After a short conversation, she hung up.

"She's not there," she told Luke.

"Who's not where?"

"Lina Porter. She's not at work. They said she's on vacation for the next week."

"Did they say where she went?"

"The receptionist didn't know."

"There's nothing on her Facebook page or anything?"

"No, not a word."

"And she's not at home, so she could have gone anywhere."

"Wait a minute!" Patricia had an idea. "We're being stupid. The husband might know where she is."

Luke rolled his eye and muttered, "We should've thought of that before." Then he nodded. "You're right. Let's try to reach – what's his name, anyway?"

"Give me a minute." Patricia turned back to her computer. "I love Facebook," she murmured as she checked the site. "Here it is. Her husband's name is Kyle. Not sure if it's the same last name, but we can start with –"

"– Kyle Porter, can I help you?" Kyle didn't recognize the number that had flashed up on his telephone screen, but who knew? He was just hoping it wasn't a scammer or robocall.
"Mr. Porter, I'm Officer Stanley, from the Malvern Police."
"Yes?" Kyle sat down slowly in his hotel room chair.
"We're trying to locate your wife. Would you happen to know where she is?"
"My wife? What's this about? Has something happened to her?"
There was a pause at the other end of the line. "No, Mr. Porter. As far as we know, she's fine. We just need to speak to her."
"About what? What's going on?"
"She may have information about an investigation we're working on, and we'd like to reach her as soon as possible."
"Well, can't you call her?" That was a stupid question, but Kyle couldn't help asking.
"She's not answering, and we've left a few messages for her, both at home and at her office."
"I – I honestly don't know where she is right now. I'm in New York on business – haven't seen Lina since I left two days ago."
"Have you talked to her?"
"A couple of texts when I got here, that's all."

[274]

"OK. If you do hear from her, please let us know right away, all right? And don't worry. As far as we know, your wife is not in any danger."

"Sure, yeah, I'll call you." Kyle ended the call and sat staring.

After a minute or two, Kyle tried Lina's number – no answer. He left a message, turned on his laptop and accessed the hotel's WiFi connection. That cop had said that *as far as they knew*, Lina was fine. But what if something had happened to her? It wasn't like her not to pick up, especially when he called. At least if he checked their online bank records, he'd know whether she'd used any of the accounts in the last couple of days. He logged on to their bank's website and started scrolling through the transactions he saw. It all looked normal enough: a fuel purchase, some clothes, groceries, the electricity bill.

Then, he checked Lina's credit card. It made him uncomfortable to do that. As a rule, he wasn't the snooping type, and he'd always respected Lina's privacy. But this might be different. It didn't take long for him to find it – an airline ticket. Why the hell would she buy an airline ticket? He picked up his telephone again, checked his log, and called the police officer who'd spoken to him.

"Thanks very much, Mr. Porter," Patricia said. "We'll follow up on this...yes, of course, we'll let you know...absolutely...Oh, and could I ask you one more question? Do you happen to know if your wife grows a plant called foxglove?... So we have your permission? ... Thanks very much." She ended the call and looked over at Luke.

"Feel like going for a ride?"

"What's up?"

"I want to check with Grant about some things. I'll be back in a few minutes, and I'll tell you on the way. Promise."

Fifteen minutes later, Patricia and Luke were in one of the police units. As soon as Patricia started the engine, Luke said, "OK, give. What are we doing?"

"Sorry, Luke. I didn't mean to be mysterious. It's just that I don't know how much time we have, and I wanted to get on the road right away. It's about Lina Porter."

"What about her?"

"I talked to her husband, Kyle. He found out she bought a plane ticket."

"To where?"

"He didn't know. We need to find that out. All he knew was that it was a flight on American Airlines. And my guess is, it's probably out of Philadelphia. But first we need to go to their house. The husband gave us the go-ahead to look on the property for foxglove, and to check the house to be sure Lina isn't hurt or worse. Says the people next door have a spare key. He's worried something might be wrong. I got the OK from Grant, too."

"Got it. And if we find foxglove?"

"Well, then we take the next step and head for the airport. Airlines won't give out anything over the phone."

After they'd gotten the spare key, Luke and Patricia got out of the car. The sound of their steps echoed in the silence as they walked towards the front yard. "We've both already checked the front yard," Luke almost whispered. Why did he feel the need to keep his voice down? There was just something about the empty house. Even the windows looked as though they were daring these interlopers to come any closer. Patricia felt it, too. She nodded and whispered, "I know, but let's get a look at those unplanted patches of soil. Just to be sure." Luke nodded back.

They went over to one of the unplanted patches of ground. Patricia bent over and looked closely. "Look," she pointed at the ground. "There's a little tiny seedling here. It's too small to tell what it is, but it could be foxglove."
"It might be. I'm no expert."
"I'm not, either, but I know they can re-seed themselves. Wait, here's another one. I'll get some of it, and we can find out what it is. Do we have any evidence bags or anything in the car?"
"I'll find something. Hang on."
Five minutes later, Luke was back. He'd found a plastic bag that would do. Patricia carefully covered the seedling with the bag, lifted it out of the ground, and closed the bag.
"Let's check the back yard, see if there's any more," Luke suggested.

The gate was locked. "We can probably get to the back yard through the house," Luke said.
"Here we go, then."
The key worked, thank God, and they were in the house within seconds. There was no sign of Lina Porter.
"Wherever she is," Patricia murmured, "she's not here."
After checking all the rooms once more, Luke and Patricia opened the sliding glass doors that led to

the back yard. The back lawn wasn't very large, but it was well-kept, and surrounded by a boxwood hedge. There were two flower beds, one on each side of the yard, and a small shed in the back corner.

"How about I take this half," Luke pointed to his right. "You can take that half."

"OK."

Each walked slowly around, looking for foxglove. After about five minutes, Patricia stopped. "Nothing here. But we've got something good with that seedling. We have to get it tested, but I'll bet it's baby foxglove."

"I think so, too."

"Guess we head to the airport. Would you call the boss? I'd better call Becky – this could take a while."

It wasn't a good time to try to get to the airport. The afternoon traffic was already backed up, and Patricia could feel her nerves getting more and more frayed. "Put some music on," she said to Luke. "Anything, as long as it's not country."

"What's wrong with country?" Patricia's glance was enough. He turned on the radio and soon found an oldies station. Good enough.

For a few minutes, neither Luke nor Patricia said anything. Elton John was singing about Bennie and the Jets, and Patricia was tapping her fingers on the steering wheel in time to the music. Luke tried Rachel Clemons' number twice, but got her voice mail both times.

"That's weird," he muttered, half to himself.

"What's weird?"

"I've tried to get Rachel Clemons on and off all afternoon, but she's not picking up. And she wasn't home when I went there."

"So she went somewhere. She'll probably be back later."

"Yeah, but without her phone?"

"That is a little odd, but it happens." Patricia didn't want to dismiss Luke's concern. All she needed was friction with him. "We can check on her again when we're done at the airport if you want."

"Yeah, OK." Luke seemed satisfied with that, and Patricia went back to trying to pick the fastest lane.

Just under an hour later, Luke and Patricia got to the Philadelphia International Airport. It took them a few minutes, but they finally found a place to park. Then, they went in search of the American Airlines desk. It took ten minutes ("I'm sorry, we don't give out passenger information...Oh, you're police officers. I see....") to convince the gate agent to confirm Lina Porter's reservation.

"Ms. Porter was reserved for Flight 325 to Chicago, leaving at 2:45 pm."

Patricia and Luke looked at each other. "Can you tell us whether she boarded that flight?" Patricia asked.

"I really shouldn't..."

"Look, this is a murder investigation," Luke said, using his, 'don't-screw-with-me' voice.

The gate agent's face paled a little. "Oh. Well..." She bit her lower lip. "Give me a second." Her fingers moved on her computer keyboard. "Here it is," she said in a slightly lower tone of voice. "She did board the plane."

"Thank you," Patricia smiled. "You've been very helpful."

"Just one more quick question," Luke said.

"Yes?" The agent's voice wasn't encouraging.

"Can you check on another passenger for me? The name is Clemons. Rachel Clemons."

"On the same flight?"

"Sorry, we're not sure."

The agent sighed, but looked back at her screen. A minute later, she said, "It looks like a Rachel Clemons was scheduled on Flight 299 to San Francisco."

"San Francisco?" Patricia mumbled. Then she shook her head a little.

Luke thanked the desk agent again. "You've really helped us out," he said, flashing his best smile. She smiled back slightly. Then, as they turned to leave the counter, the agent said, "In case it matters, that itinerary to San Francisco has a stop in Chicago. Passengers change planes there."

Fifteen

She looked out the window as the plane touched down on the runway. All she had to do was get out of the airport. A train, a bus, and a little walking and she'd be in Palatine. It would have been easier and much quicker to rent a car, but even she knew not to leave a more of a credit card trail than she had to. As the passengers shuffled off the plane and onto the jetway, she thought through her plan again. It would all come together. She hadn't wanted it to be like this, but there really was no other choice. And in the end, she'd be appreciated.

She finally got to the train ticket kiosks, bought the ticket she needed, and went through to the train station to wait. Funny, there was no reason for anyone to notice her, but she couldn't help wondering if anyone did. Not as far as she could see, but she'd made sure to be as inconspicuous as she could. When the train came, she got on board. In less than an hour, she'd be in Palatine. And this time, she'd get it right.

Patricia ended the call and slid her telephone back into her pocket. "Grant says it's worth it to call Palatine. Just to be sure," she told Luke.
"You have a point," Luke agreed. "And we've got both of those women going to Chicago."
"We can't do much more here. Let's call Palatine and then get back to the station."

Caroline Drackmann slowly put the telephone back in its cradle. She wasn't usually one to panic easily. Over the years, she'd found it was much better to take a cautious approach. There was no need to frighten people without a good reason. But too much caution could cost lives, too. And that detective from Pennsylvania had seemed pretty sure. She took a breath and then looked at her watch. It wouldn't hurt to go ten minutes out of her way – just run by the house and make sure everything was OK. She'd told Victor Wagner and his wife that she would check in with them, anyway, so why not?

Her mind made up, Drackmann shut down her computer, made a face as she took a last swallow of cold coffee, picked up her keys and bag, and left. As she headed for her car, she thought about whether or not to call the Wagners and let them know she was coming. In the end, she decided against it. It didn't make sense to worry them unless there was a compelling reason.

Victor Wagner pulled the pan of chicken and rice out of the oven. Syd insisted she was fine, but he didn't want her lifting anything heavier than a piece of paper right now. "Besides," he would tell her, "You'll be making up for it in lost sleep once the baby comes." He carried the pan over to the couple's small dining table and put it next to the serving spoon that Syd had left there when she set the table. "It's ready," he called out. Syd soon appeared, carrying two glasses of iced tea. She put them one at each place, and she and Victor sat down to eat.

"So, how'd it go today?" Syd asked.
"Nothing much new," Victor said as he started to put a forkful of rice in his mouth. He swallowed and

then added, "They're talking about adding a few new positions, which would be great."

Syd nodded. "It'd be nice for you to get back to doing just one person's job."

Victor was about to answer when they heard a knock at the door. Syd shrugged and Victor got up to see who was there.

"Yes?" Victor asked when he opened the door. He didn't recognize the woman who stood there, although something about her was familiar.

"Hello," she smiled. "I'm conducting a survey of local voters to find out some of the issues that matter to you. Could you answer a few questions?"

Victor thought about his dinner, getting colder by the minute. "Look, I'm sorry," he said, "I was just about to eat. Can you come back another time?"

"Oh, this will only take a minute. I promise."

"This isn't a good time. You'll have to come back."

"All right, then, I'll do that."

Victor felt a sting on his arm as he turned to go back inside. Damned wasps! He'd get an ice pack as soon as he could. He didn't see the woman step off the porch and turn to leave.

That had gone much better than she had expected it would. In just a few minutes, she'd be back at the bus stop. Then it would be just a bus and a train ride back to the airport, and she'd be gone. As she picked up her bag and started down the street, she thought through everything. It had been hard – much harder than it seemed from TV and books. But she'd done the right thing. She would have to live with what happened, but she'd really had no choice at all.

"I'll get it," Syd said as the doorbell rang. "You lie down and rest."

Victor nodded and lay back down on the living room sofa. Whatever it was, it was making him feel awful. He'd never been allergic to bee or wasp stings before, but there was a first time for everything. After a minute or two, a wave of nausea hit. He struggled to his feet and hurried for the bathroom. He could hear Syd talking to someone as he cleaned himself up.

"…just as a precaution," Drackmann said as Victor struggled back into the living room. Syd turned to him. "Honey, Officer Drackmann stopped by to see if everything's OK."

Victor sat heavily on the sofa. "Sorry," he muttered. "I got stung by a wasp or something, and I think I'm having an allergic reaction. I tried to take some Benadryl, but I can't keep anything down."

"You ought to get checked out," Drackmann said. "Just to be on the safe side."

"She's right," Syd agreed. "I'll take you over to the urgent care place." Then, she looked over at Drackmann. "Except for the wasp sting, we're fine. Nobody's been bothering us or anything, and there've been no strangers hanging around. I don't mean to be rude, but I really want to get Victor over to the doctor."

"Of course."

"Wait a minute," Victor mumbled. "That lady. The one taking the poll. She came to the door." Then came another wave of nausea. He got up, barely making it to the bathroom this time.

"What lady?" Drackmann asked Syd.

"I didn't see her. Victor answered the door. It was about an hour and a half ago. Then he came back in and said she was taking some political survey, and he'd only be a minute. We were eating dinner. Anyway, by the time he got back to the door, she was gone." Then, the realization hit her. "That wasn't a pollster, was it?"

"We can't tell that now. Let's get your husband some medical help, and we'll go from there." Victor nearly staggered back into the living room. "I don't think this is just an allergic reaction," he said weakly, and slumped into the nearest chair. Drackmann made a decision. "We'd better not wait through the urgent care process. I'm going to get you some paramedics."

Fifteen minutes later, Victor was secured on a gurney, being wheeled to the back of the ambulance. Drackmann watched as Syd got in, too. She pounded her hand against her car as the ambulance roared off. She'd been supposed to take care of this family, and now it looked as though this nut, whoever it was, had struck again. *Damnit!* There should have been some way to prevent this. Beating herself up wasn't going to do any good, though. She took a deep breath and thought for a minute. The medical people would do everything they could for Victor Wagner. She'd check on him later. For now, she was better off trying to catch the person who did this.

The police in Pennsylvania had given Drackmann two names. Both of the women had gone through O'Hare, which meant there was a good chance they'd leave that way, too. It took a few calls (including one to her supervisor to clear her plan), but Drackmann got the airport authorities to agree to cooperate. Just in case, she also got permission to alert the people at Chicago Midway, too. With both major airports covered, there wasn't much else to do at the moment but wait. It made her feel restless, but there was no sense in her driving all over greater Chicago looking for two people who could be just about anywhere.

Rachel walked towards the departure gate at O'Hare. Just a little while now and they'd be calling her flight to San Francisco. Then, she'd be out of this airport and on her way to Napa. She thought through everything as she waited for the boarding call, but, no, there was nothing she'd forgotten. There weren't a lot of seats available at the gate, but she found one and settled herself to wait. Her scalp prickled just a little as she noticed a couple of uniformed security agents going to the gate desk. One of them glanced her way and she looked down at the magazine she'd brought with her, pretending to read it. But no, it didn't seem like either of the agents was paying attention to her. She took a deep breath and went back to her magazine, this time actually trying to focus. It didn't work. She'd never had an easy time traveling, and without Ron, it was even worse. Ron. He wouldn't have cared about the security people. Then, a minute or two later, she heard an announcement from the desk: "Rachel Clemons, Rachel Clemons, please come to the desk at Gate H8. American Airlines paging Rachel Clemons. Please come to the desk at Gate H8."

The next few minutes were almost surreal. It was as though someone else who looked just like Rachel went up to the desk and was pulled aside by the security agents.

"We need you to come with us, please," one of them said. The taller one, with glasses and a small beard.

"Why? What's this about?" Rachel asked.

"The police have a few questions for you. Let's go this way, please." That was the shorter one, clean shaven, with short, blond hair.

"Questions about what? What is this about?" Then, after a second or two. "I'm going to miss my flight."

"This way, please," the shorter security officer repeated. No facial expression, just the words. Rachel paused for a moment, then picked up her carry-on bag and handbag and followed the security guards. A few people looked up, too interested in what was going on to be polite.

A short walk down past a few gates, then through two doors and into a small room with nothing but a few chairs and a small table. Beard waved her to a seat. "Have a seat, please. The police will be here shortly." Then, he left. Blond Hair stood impassively by the door. There was no sound except for occasional muffled footsteps going by outside. After about ten minutes, the door opened, and a police officer came in. Blond Hair nodded and left the room.

The officer said, "Are you Rachel Clemons?"

"Yes, I am. What's this all about? Why am I being held here?"

"I'm Officer Drackmann. I'd like to talk to you about an incident that happened in Palatine earlier this evening."

"Palatine? I don't even know where that is. What are you talking about?"

"Can you tell me where you've been this afternoon and evening?"

"In a plane! I left Philadelphia at 3:30, landed here about an hour ago, and now I'm here."

"Could I see your ticket, please?"

Rachel swallowed hard. This was getting more and more like a nightmare. She pulled her telephone out of her handbag, activated it, and accessed her mobile boarding pass. Then, she passed it over to Drackmann, who looked at it closely. Drackmann handed the telephone back, and Rachel put it triumphantly into her handbag.

"You see? I had nothing to do with whatever it is that you're investigating. Why are you harassing me, anyway? I don't even live in the area!"

Drackmann paused for a moment. "I'm sorry. But –"

"You're sorry? You're *sorry*? You treat me like a criminal, you make me miss my flight, and you're sorry about it?"

"I know you're upset, but we're investigating an attempted murder – it'll be a murder if he doesn't make it – and we have reason to think you might know the victim. His name is Victor Wagner."

Rachel felt the anger start to fade. Should she say anything? Would it do her any good to lie? Probably not, since the police at home already knew. "I don't know him," she sighed. "We've never met. But I know who he is." Then it occurred to her. "Someone tried to kill him? Why?"

"It's too soon to know exactly what happened," Drackmann hedged. "Right now, we're looking for answers."

"I'm sorry, but I can't help you. As I say, I don't know him. And anyway, I couldn't have tried to kill him. I was in the airplane, and then here. But…I mean, is he OK?"

"It's too early to say. He's at the hospital, and they're doing what they can."

"I hope he'll make it."

Drackmann stood up. "Let's get you back to the gate desk."

Rachel looked at her watch. "I've already missed my flight."

"We'll get you on another one."

Drackmann escorted Rachel back to the gate desk and explained the situation to the agent. Twenty minutes, three calls, and dozens of keystrokes later, Rachel was booked on a new flight to San Francisco. It meant another layover, and she wouldn't get to Napa until late, but she would get there. Drackmann was turning to leave when they both heard the noise.

"Somebody's upset," Drackman murmured. Then she saw Rachel's face. "What? What is it?"

"I would have sworn that was my sister, Lina. But it couldn't be. Why would she be here?"

The voice was getting closer. "You can't hold me here like this! You're violating my rights!" A police officer came into view. With him was a woman who was nearly spluttering. He said nothing as they walked down the hall.

"Oh my God! It *is* Lina!" Rachel gasped. She hurried after the pair.

"I keep telling you," Lina insisted. "I had nothing to do with anything. I don't even live in Illinois. And I don't know anyone named Victor Wagner. Why

[289]

would I want to kill someone I don't even know?"
She stared across the table in the small room, her
eyes daring the officer to question her.

"OK, let's start at the beginning. You got into
Chicago at…what time?"

"About 3:30."

"And what time is your flight out of Chicago?"

"I'm *supposed* to board in half an hour, so I hope
you'll keep this short!"

"So you were only planning to be in Chicago for a
few hours? And you flew from Philadelphia? To be
honest, that doesn't make a lot of sense to me."

"Listen, Officer…" Lina looked at the police
officer's nametag "…Robertson. I'm not breaking
any laws by being here, and I don't have to give you
chapter and verse on what I do with my time!"

Robertson leaned back a little in his chair. "It won't
be hard to check up on when you left the airport and
returned. We can find out where you went, too. You
might as well just tell me the story yourself."

Robertson was right, of course. Lina sat silently for
a minute, chewing her bottom lip. She looked down
at the table, then up again. She started to say
something, then changed her mind when the door
burst open.

"Lina, there you are! What are you doing here?"

"Excuse me," Robertson said. "This is a private
interview. You can't come in here."

"Officer, this is my sister!"

"Rachel, don't worry. It's all OK." Lina's face
hardened a little as she looked back at Robertson.
"I'm not saying anything more to you!"

"Lina, what is going on?"

Drackmann appeared just behind Rachel. "Come on, Mrs. Clemons. We should get back to your gate and let Officer Robertson do his job."

Rachel turned around. "You know him? He's working with you, isn't he?"

"Yes, we're working together on this case."

Rachel turned back to Lina. "Why are you even involved?" Then she stopped. Her face paled and her eyes widened a little. "You knew about Victor. Did – did you have something to do with this?"

Lina looked away.

"You did! Why? Why would you want to kill him?"

"Don't you get it?" Lina looked up at Rachel, and a little strength came back into her face. "I did it for you! I'm trying to take care of you, like I always have. Victor and his wife could get everything, and I couldn't let that happen. I had to make sure you and Jason were protected. You ought to be grateful."

"Protected from what? Victor hasn't tried to get anything from me. He hasn't even contacted me."

It was as though Drackmann and Robertson weren't even there. Lina stood up and faced her sister. "Ron was going to change his will, or maybe you didn't know that. But I did." Her words started to come faster. "I stopped by one day. You weren't there, but Ron was. He was on the phone, and I knew something was wrong, so when he hung up, I asked him. He told me he'd just been talking to his son, and at first, I thought he meant Jason, but of course, he didn't. Then he told me about Victor. He begged me to keep it secret, that he'd tell you when he was ready. All right, I said. I'll keep quiet for now, but you have to tell her. He promised he would, and I thought that would be the end."

Rachel groaned, "Oh, God! Ron!" and slumped into chair. "You killed Ron?"

"I had no choice," Lina insisted as her eyes filled with tears. "Ron told me that as soon as he could, he was going to change his will to include Victor. I couldn't let him steal your money that way. I had to do something, didn't I? It wasn't hard, really," she went on. "I went to the coffee shop. I asked him – pleaded with him – to forget about Victor Wagner. He said no, Victor was his son. You would understand, he said. I figured he'd say that, so I had what I needed with me. When he turned around to tell the waitress to bring the bill, I took care of it. Don't cry, it's all going to be OK. You and Jason will get everything."

Rachel put her arms on the table and rested her head on them. Drackmann could hear her sobs as Robertson took Lina out of the room.

Sixteen

"That was Palatine," Patricia said as she put down her telephone. She and Luke had gone back to the police department to update Grant on their trip to Philadelphia. Now they were sitting in his office.

"What'd they say?" Grant wanted to know.

"It was Lina Porter. She also just confessed to killing Ronald Clemons."

"And we almost missed her completely," Luke muttered, annoyed with himself.

"We got there. That's what's important. Good call on the seedling, by the way." Grant reassured them. "We'll get the official results back in a few days, but it looks like foxglove."

"So now we extradite her?" Patricia asked.

"We'll work that out with Palatine. For now, she's being held there until we get the details ironed out. She'll probably be tried twice. Once there for murder and attempted murder if Wagner doesn't live, and two counts of attempted murder if he does. And once here."

"I still don't quite get it," Patricia mused. "She kills one person and tries to kill another. She doesn't get money out of it or anything, and she wasn't threatened. She did it because she thought she was taking care of her sister. It's hard to get my mind around that."

"That's one thing I've learned," Grant said. "You never know what will make a person kill. In her mind, she was protecting her younger sister."

There was silence for a bit as Luke and Patricia processed what Grant had said. Luke shook his head a bit, and then looked over at Patricia. "What's the story on Victor Wagner?"

"Palatine said he's in the hospital, and they're hoping they got to him in time. They'll call when they know something."

"All right, you two," Grant straightened up. "Get out of here." He grinned, and added, "You've done enough damage for one day. Go have a drink. You've earned it."

"Mind if I take a raincheck? There's something else I have to do."

"Oh, my God, you're blushing," Luke teased. "Come on, out with it. What do you have to do that's so important?"

"None of your damned business, smartass," Patricia shot back. "I'll tell you tomorrow."

Grant shrugged, and he and Luke looked at each other as she left the office.

How long had she been sitting in this same seat? Rachel didn't know. It felt like hours, but it might not have been that long. At some point, she would have to get up and go somewhere. She'd heard her name called a few times over the airport's PA system, urging her to go to her boarding gate. She hadn't moved, though. There was no way she could get on that flight. Not now. But she was going to have to do something. She ought to talk to Kyle. Someone should tell Kyle. But it wasn't going to be Rachel – she couldn't bring herself to think about that. Not Lina. Not her big sister. But it was. She could feel the beginnings of nausea as she let that thought sink in. Think of something else – anything. And get up from this chair. Jason would have to know, too. Yes, Jason. That would be a place to start. Her stomach started to settle a little as she swallowed and tried to focus on Jason. Nodding slowly to herself, she pulled her telephone from her handbag and cleared her throat. Then, she tapped on Jason's telephone number.

"How are you, Mom? Did you make it to San Francisco OK?"

"No, there's been – something's happened. I have to talk to you. It's about Aunt Lina."

"Aunt Lina? Is she OK?"

Rachel swallowed. "It's a long story, and I'd rather tell you in person. Would you mind if I had a change of plans and came to Boston for a visit?"

"Um – yeah, sure. Mom, what's wrong?"

"I promise, I'll tell you about it when I get there. For now, don't panic. I'm not in danger or anything."

"If you say so."

"OK. I'll see what I can do about a flight and text you as soon as I have the details."

"All right."

Syd Wagner sat next to her husband's hospital bed. Nobody told you how depressing it was to listen to the whirr of the monitoring machines. Anyone who could possibly think that hospitals were restful places had obviously never been in one. For one thing, there was the constant flow of traffic by the door: people walking; people pushing gurneys or carts; wheelchairs; and, sometimes, conversations. For another, they never let a patient alone to rest. Syd could swear that someone had been in Victor's room every twenty or thirty minutes to do something.

The worst thing was that no-one would tell her anything much. "He's in good shape and he's

young," one of the doctors told her. "He has a good chance." But even that doctor wouldn't tell her straight out whether Victor would be all right. They kept hedging their bets and saying those vague things like, "We're doing everything we can."
"I know that," she'd responded at one point. "I just want to know if he's going to make it!" But nobody would be definite.

Now, Syd leaned back in the visitor's chair and tried to stretch out her legs. There was nothing to prop her slightly swollen feet and ankles on, so she had to make do with resting them on her handbag. She listened for a minute to Victor's breathing and to the machines, and then closed her eyes. She'd almost nodded off when the baby kicked. Her eyes flew open and she looked across at Victor. He moved his head a little on the pillow and his right hand plucked at the blanket, but he didn't wake up. Still, he was alive and breathing, and she'd definitely seen him move. That was something in itself for right now. She took a few breaths, settled herself as much as she could, and closed her eyes again.

An hour later, Victor's eyelids flickered, and he slowly opened his eyes. He blinked a few times, then turned his head to look at Syd, who was still dozing. Her hair had fallen partway over her face, and her right shoe had come off. The left shoe dangled from her foot. He watched her for a few minutes as he tried to orient himself. She must have sensed him watching, because she slowly opened her own eyes. When she saw that he was awake, she straightened up a little, and then slowly stood up, gripping the arms of the chair for support. She

[296]

walked over to the bed and sat on the edge of it, taking Victor's hand in hers. She blinked back tears and murmured "It's about time you woke up. It's your night to do the dishes."

"So, this is it, then," Greg looked over the top of his wine glass at Denise, who was toying with her untouched shrimp.
"I think so." Her eyes met his, and he saw what he'd expected. Not much of anything. "I'm sorry," she said.
"No, don't say that, because you aren't."
Now those eyes narrowed a little. "Give me some credit, Greg. I don't want to hurt you."
"I know that. I don't mean you're not sorry for that. I mean you're not sorry for taking that job with the state senator and moving, and you're not sorry you're leaving Mid-Atlantic, and you're not sorry that we're ending things because of it."
Denise lowered her eyes as his point hit home. "I can't pass up opportunities when they come around."
"That's what I mean. You're driven. I think you give up too much along the way. I just hope it's all worth it when you get where you're going."
Greg got up from the table, a little surprised that it didn't really hurt to leave. Besides, he had plenty to occupy him, like trying to find a new job. Denise had cost him enough.

When Patricia got home, she found Becky curled up under a blanket on the sofa, watching something on TV. "You made it," Becky yawned as she sat up.
"Yeah, finally. Sorry I'm getting in so late."

Becky put up a hand. "Don't be. I'm learning that's part of being with a cop – the hours. Besides, you called, so at least I knew."

Patricia sat on the sofa next to Becky. "I try to remember. I know it's not easy being a cop's partner." She was quiet for a minute, and Becky looked over at her.

"You OK?"

Patricia took a deep breath. "I know I'm not always easy to be with, especially with my job. But you're happy?"

Becky took her hand. "I am. Why would you even ask? What's wrong?"

"Nothing's wrong." Patricia turned so she could see Becky's face. "I'm just wondering…do you think you could do it forever?"

"Do what?"

"Be with a cop?"

"What are you talking about?"

Patricia took Becky's other hand. "I'm asking you to marry me. Will you?"

"You mean it?"

It was surprising how easy it was to answer that. "Yeah, I do."

"Then yes. I do. I mean I will. I mean –" Then she laughed a little and wiped a tear from her right eye. "God, that sounded stupid. Yes, I will marry you."

Click. Patricia could almost hear the sound of something falling into place as she and Becky hugged.

The next morning, Emma Yeats looked around Mid-Atlantic's conference room. The box of pastries she'd set on the table was open, and the coffee was almost done. She slowly took her seat as Trent Rakins walked in. "Morning, Emma," he flashed her that "sales pitch" smile and winked as he sat down. Next to come in was Wade Messner, who smiled at Emma and ignored Trent as he took his seat. Everyone looked up when a tall woman with medium-length, wavy brown hair and a navy-blue tailored suit joined them. Trent stood up.

"Folks," he said, "I'd like to introduce you to Susan LeMont, who's joining our sales force. She's here today to get a sense of how we do things around here."

Susan looked around at everyone and half-smiled at the murmured greetings.

"Susan," Trent said, "You're going to have a great career here. We're reaching out to all sorts of new clients, so there'll be lots of opportunities for you to connect. In fact, we're going to be heading in a whole new direction that's going to make us great. Ron Clemons was a fine leader, but it's time for us to break out with some new ideas, and that's just what we're going to do."

Wade couldn't help smiling a little to himself as Trent went on. Next week, Jason Clemons would be spending a few days at the company to familiarize himself with how things were done. If he was anything like his father, Trent wouldn't get very far with his plans. Now, he silently toasted Ron's memory as Trent finished up: "Let's hop to it, everyone."

About the Author

Margot Kinberg is a mystery novelist with many years of experience in higher education. Don't miss her other novels, *Publish or Perish*, *B-Very Flat*, *Past Tense*, and *Downfall!* Connect with Margot on Facebook.

CPSIA information can be obtained
at www.ICGtesting.com
Printed in the USA
FSHW011835010520
69833FS